THE MYSTIFYING MURDER IN MARION, OHIO

Contents

INTRODUCTION

Photo by Mike Perry

Marion, Ohio, in 1919 was, as little towns go, probably a typical little town, with its share of 1919 things going on. However, in doing research on one topic, I discovered related events that gained my interest—a tragic event that precipitated the second set of tragic events. As time has passed, it seems to me that the second set of events, in retrospect, was probably more sinister than the first. But having said that, I intend to explore the first crime then, in the process, take another look at the second, as well as look at connecting stories. I will do this by reviewing both events as reported in the *Marion Daily Star*, Marion, Ohio's, leading newspaper of 1919, as well as other newspapers in Ohio and other parts of the USA. Please remember that, for the most part, I will be copying news articles exactly as they appeared in the *Marion Daily Star* and others, and that these stories reflect those times and what was thought of then as the proper use of our language.

Before we get to Marion in 1919, let's look at what was happening in our nation and the world in 1919.

The first trans-Atlantic flight in world history occurred in 1919, on June 14, when Captain John Alcock and Lieutenant Arthur White flew from Newfoundland to Ireland in sixteen hours.

On the national scene, the eighteenth amendment was passed, which became the only amendment (so far) to be repealed. This was the Volstead Act, which of course was prohibition and gave rise to Al Capone (bad guy) and Eliot Ness (good guy.)

The Treaty of Versailles ending World War I was signed on June 28, 1919.

Shemp Howard of the Three Stooges, and Boris Karloff, who was made famous by Frankenstein, made their film debuts in 1919.

And Babe Ruth was pitching for the Boston Red Sox, where he set a record for most consecutive scoreless innings pitched in a world series, a record that lasted until 1961, when it was broken by Whitey Ford of the New York Yankees.

PROLOGUE

To set the stage for our story, I want to review for you some facts about Marion, Ohio.

From the *Marion Daily Star* issue on September 6, 1919, we have this headline: "Ten Convictions in Decade in Thirty-Two Homicides."

In the past ten years in Marion county, there have been thirty-two homicides according to statistics in common pleas court. The largest number of homicides in one year was in 1917 when there were seven.

In 1909, there were no homicides and in 1914 only one. There were two homicides in each of the years 1910, 1911, and 1915. A peculiar feature is that in the years when there were a number of homicides, there were few suicides, while in the years when there were few homicides, there were a number of suicides.

In 1909, when there were no homicides, there were four suicides, and in 1917, when there were seven homicides, there were no suicides. In 1914, when there was but one homicide there were six suicides.

During the past ten years, 114 persons have been killed by accident according to statistics. In 1917, there was the greatest number of people killed by accident, the total that year being twenty-seven. The fewest number of persons to be accidentally killed was in 1909 when there were two.

Of the thirty-two homicides committed in ten years, there have been but six convictions for first-degree murder. There has been but one acquittal for first-degree murder in the same period. The total number convicted of second-degree murder during the same period was three with four acquitted on the same charge. On a charge of manslaughter, there has been but one conviction in the past ten years. (Following this story appeared a chart showing the above statistics. The chart follows.)

Here Are the Statistics

1. The statistics for the past ten years for homicides, suicides, and fatal accidents are as follows:

Year	Homicide	Suicide	Accident
1909	0	4	2
1910	2	2	5
1911	2	3	9
1912	4	6	16
1913	5	6	12
1914	1	6	9
1915	2	2	9
1916	6	9	13
1917	7	0	27
1918	3	4	12
	32	42	114

Another item of interest for me is speculating about the categorization of some of these figures. A friend mentioned to me that the discrepancy in suicides and murders and accidental deaths might be partly due to people getting murdered and that murder getting covered up by making it appear to be an accident or scaring witnesses to give false testimony. And when you read about the Black Hand and its influence, you may agree.

The next set of facts that I believe are interesting are those that show Marion's population. In 1910, according to the US Census, Marion's population stood at 18,232, then grew to an estimated 29,171 according to the Newspaper Feature Bureau as printed in the *Marion Daily Star* on a Saturday, August 30, 1919. This growth in population most likely was due to the growing industrial base in our fair city. And

I know personally that my grandfather Reid came to Marion from Cambridge, Ohio, in 1915 to work in a steel mill.

And finally, some information that may have had an effect on the mind-set of Marionites and the conviction rate for murder cases in Marion. So we begin with chapter 1.

CHAPTER 1

The Black Hand

Something I had heard about Marion, but mostly thought, was simply attempts to glamorize Marion's past were references to the mob or the Mafia, but I didn't give a lot of credibility to those remarks. Then in looking at material for this book, I discovered that there were indeed members of this organization in good old Marion. And this presence may give some insight to criminal activities in Marion during these years, which were very active between 1900 and 1925 or so.

The Black Hand was mainly a group of Italian immigrants who specialized in extortion, but were also involved in many other nefarious activities. The "La Mano Nera" threatened folks with arson, murder, kidnapping, or simply bodily harm to obtain payoffs. And if the victim did not pay off, the threats would come true. And any persons having knowledge of the crimes committed would be warned to stay quiet or suffer the consequences. So most people remained silent.

The first article I want to use to show the impact and importance of the Black Hand in Marion appeared in *The Marion Daily Mirror* on June 8, 1909, and had these headlines. The first in bold capital letters stated that "MARION IS HEADQUARTERS FOR BLACK HAND GANG." This headline was followed by "This is the Claim Made by Federal Officers" then "TWO ARRESTS ARE MADE" and "Sam Lima and Joe Rizo are Now in Custody" and finally, "Other Arrests will Probably be Made within a Few Days—Big Sensations Promised."

That Marion is the headquarters of a band of "Black Hand" workers, who have been using the mails to send threatening letters to intended victims, promising dire vengeance if the society's demands are not complied with, is the declaration of special detectives of the post office department who today arrested two local fruit merchants.

Sam Lima and Joe Rizo are the two Italians arrested this morning by the federal officers. It is expected that at least five other arrests will be made in this locality during the next few days.

The officers, J. F. Oldfield, E. F. Hutchens and R. C. Rosford entered the Lima store on North Main street this morning. After placing the proprietor under arrest they searched the store and found a large bundle of letters which will, the detectives claim, divulge many of the plots either planned or carried out by the alleged blackmailers.

Lima, his wife and the others in the store, seem to be unusually excited when the officers took charge. It was not long however, before they changed front entirely and assisted the officers in making the search. Several of the men who make the Lima store their headquarters were not to be found but the officers are on the lookout for them and expect to get them before they can leave town.

It is the contention of the post office authorities that Italians, living in Marion and many of the surrounding cities, have been systematically working together for several years. They say the plan is to send several threatening letters to a merchant, man of wealth, generally an American, but sometimes of their own race, demanding a large sum of money for immunity from the vengeance of the "Black Hand." It is claimed that in many cases the money has been paid without any information being gleaned either by the public or by the police, the victim being warned that publication of the letters would mean certain death.

Whether any real deeds of violence can be traced to this band the authorities refuse to state, claiming that when the whole band is under arrest the details of one of the biggest captures made in recent years will be unfolded. Several arrests have already been made throughout this section of the state and more are to follow.

The officers state that neither Lima nor Rizo are the ring leaders. But they claim that he two leaders of the band live here and will be under arrest in the near future.

It is said that the arrests are the results of months of labor by numerous detectives of the post office department. Mail between parties supposed to be in the band has been intercepted, read, and then the envelope carefully resealed and forwarded to their destinations to prevent suspicion that the authorities were cognizant of the guilty parties.

Lima is being held incommunicado, at the city prison, and Rizo is locked up in the county jail. The case will come to trial in the United States court at Toledo to which place the prisoners will shortly be removed. In the meantime a close watch will be kept upon them to prevent any attempt to liberate them.

Another item from the *Marion Daily Mirror* on a Wednesday, June 9, 1909, illustrates the criminal organization. The large, leading headline says in bold capital letters, "MORE EVIDENCE IS SECURED AGAINST SUSPECTED BLACK HAND." This was followed by a smaller headline, "Members of the Gang Which is Supposed to Have Its Headquarters in Marion are Arrested in Other Cities." Then this lead in bold print: "Two More Local Italians are Taken into Custody and One of those Arrested Tuesday is Released_ John Amicon Gives the Officers the Tip Which Leads to the Arrests_Paper and Ink Such as Used by the Writer of the Black Hand Letters Found When John Lima's Place was Searched Adds to the Belief that Marion was the Headquarters_Murder of Luca Giofritta May Yet be Traced to the Black Hand."

With the round-up of practically all of the gang of the alleged "Black Hand" members, who are charged with hundreds of blackmailing attempts, some of which were successful, the inspectors of the post office department, Tuesday night divulged much of the information they have secured during six long months of labor on the case.

Tuesday morning the inspectors arrested Sam Lima, the North Main street fruit dealer and Joe Rizzo. Later developments proved that Joe Rizzo had no part in the conspiracies and he was released. Last night the officers arrested Sam Z. Rizzo, whose real name is said to be Salvatore Rizzo, Salvatore Bataglia and Antonio Vierio. The men are being held here awaiting the arrival of the United States Marshal from Cleveland, when they will be taken to Toledo for trial in the United States courts. While the work was carried on by the trio of officers Tuesday, other post office sleuths were working at Dennison, Bellefontaine, Columbus and other places over the state, rounding up practically all of the gang.

The specific offense in which all these men are said to be implicated is the attempt to extort $10,000 from John Amicon and Charles Amicon, of the John Amicon Fruit company, of Columbus. The whole raid is the result of the confession made by one of the members when arrested some time ago in Pittsburg. Since that time several hundred letters, passing between members of the gang, have been intercepted and much valuable evidence secured. It is claimed that Marion has been the headquarters of the gang and that Sam or Salvatore Lima is known as the leader. Hundreds of others are affiliated with Lima in this particular gang. Other societies are also affiliated and are known to have loaned men for certain deeds the society wanted performed. As far as the inspectors have been able to learn only Italians and Sicilians have been molested.

In the raids made Tuesday much evidence has been procured. The full extent of this will not be known until the contents to several mails sacks are fully translated. It is claimed that the members of the gang have recently sent hundreds of dollars to Italy. Salvatore Lima received all of the tribute paid by hundreds of Italians throughout this part of the United States. There is no evidence that he divided with any of the others but it seems that most of the gang paid tribute to him.

The band was as the Society of the Banana. Lima was at its head and received all of the money. He recently sent large sums to alleged confederates in Italy.

At the direction of Lima, conventions were held here and in other places members of the band attending from all over Ohio, Pittsburg and Western Pennsylvania. At these meetings reports were made upon Italians from whom money was to be demanded. The case of those who refused to pay were considered and the inspectors of the post office department believe that Lima passed judgement on those who would not pay. He is also thought to have designated the member or members of the band who were to deal out vengeance to those who failed to pay tribute to the Mafia. Among Italians the band has been known as the "Black Hand," despite the fancy name sometimes attributed to it. There seems to be no evidence that Lima is the national head of the society but authorities rather believe that he is the head of a band that covers a certain portion of the United States. That he has been in communication with the other leaders both in this country and in Italy is certain.

There is generally an organization wherever Italians are located in any number. The leader, chosen by the band, is supreme authority and there is a penalty of death for failure to obey his mandates. In every place searched Tuesday the inspectors found large sums of money but they did not molest it.

The gang was well organized. Its demands were accompanied by threats of violence. In some cases where money demanded was not paid the threats were carried out.

In January, Mrs. John Amicon, wife of the Columbus and Marion fruit dealer, found in the rear of the house a dynamite bomb and fuse, wrapped with one of the letters, demanding $10,000 from her husband.

Many Columbus Italians are among those who received the threatening letters and in some instances bombs and other significant threats. Many in Columbus paid weekly or monthly tribute, the amount of which has not been learned, as yet. The post office inspectors are inclined to connect the numerous knife fights among the Italians here with the operation of the band and they believe the murder of Luca Guifritta, which went unavenged, was among the operations of this band of "Black Handers."

The Mafia is also charged with assassinations and deeds of violence in Bellefontaine, Cincinnati, Dennison and in fact, throughout Ohio, Pennsylvania and even in more different places.

After demands for money had been ignored an attempt was made in April, 1908 to blow up the home of Agostino Glennarimo, in Columbus. Dynamite was placed in a stairway and exploded at three a. m., breaking every window in the house. Glennarimo then left for Italy accompanied as far as New York by Sergeant Vic Churches, of the Columbus police department. While in his native land he received a letter mailed in that country, renewing the demand. The letter, like all the others written by the band, was written in Italian. Black Hand letters written in Italian in many parts of the country, in the hands of post office inspectors, are written by the same person, with the same kind of ink and on the same kind of paper. In the raid here Tuesday ink and paper were found, which are identical with that used in making the demands. The letter received by Glennarimo corresponds with those written here. Most of the letters received throughout this section were mailed in Pittsburg, where the money was to be paid. It is believed that they were written in this city and passed along to many different messengers before they were mailed. In this work Italians in Bellefontaine, Dennison and many other places were involved. The same system was used in following intended victims to remote places.

Postal authorities have been working on this case for many months. Over a score of sleuths have aided in the hunt. They have been aided by Italian secret spies. F. P. Dimaio, superintendent of the Pinkertons, has been working with the inspectors and helped them make the arrests.

Dimaio probably has more knowledge of the operations of the lawless Italian gang in America than any other living man. He has helped to break up and imprison members of many gangs in the country. At Columbus Tuesday at midnight the postal inspectors, who left here on the Hocking train at 7:15, went to the home of Salvatore Ventola, expecting to find documents connecting him with the attempts to extort money from the Amicons. The man was not arrested as the search proved fruitless. Some important arrests are expected in Columbus as a result of the information furnished by Ventola.

A Sample of the Letters
The following translation of one of the letters is a sample of all:

> Dear John Amicon
> We have sent you several letters. We have put dynamite behind your door and you are death. Ugly wretch. You need not lament if when you do not expect it, it will cost you your life. Already our band has you down in the register of the dead. We have arrived at the time and already two of us are under obligations to kill you even though you are guarded by a thousand police. Take the street as your friend Lieutenant Petrosino did. Ugly wretch that you are, that you content yourself with trying to avoid payment of the money, $10,000 by the blood of God we are back of you. We have learned your store

and you will be accosted when you do not expect it, the sight of two dagger thrusts and you will sleep forever. One thing I tell you. No one can belong to our band who has not killed 10 persons. We have killed kings and emperors. Consider a fly like you! No! No! Do not think it.

We know that you are rich and you must give up some blood. If you wish to avert your death, you will search for an honorable person to come to Pittsburg and while he is searching for us, he will be found. We advise you that if you go to the police, you can count yourself deadthat is, you die first.

Wretch! Do your duty without the police and it will be well. Either money or your life! In a short time you will see that we know how to do it. Soon you will bear the cross.

At the bottom of the letter is the signature of the Black Hand under a big ugly dagger on either side of which are the warnings, "Die wretch" and "Your place!" The writing is on both sides of one sheet.

Practically, all the secrets of the operations from Lima are in the hands of the inspectors. One of the members of the Black Hand when arrested made a complete confession to Detective Dimaio, revealing all that he knew. This furnished the basis for much of the work that preceded the arrests of yesterday and give the government agents all the secrets and information.

After the Monday conference in the office of Postmaster Krumm, the inspectors scattered to several cities where members of the organization are located. The list of arrests is far from complete. Before the work stops, probably a score or more will be brought to trial in the federal courts. Chief Inspector Holmes of Cincinnati discussing the case on Tuesday said, "The proof we have found against the Marion gang convinces us that they have worked their games successfully on many Italians, principally well-to-do Sicilians. We have not found where they went after a single American. They meant business when they made demands of money. If their demands were ignored they resorted to the bomb to either bring their victim to time or to avenge a persistent refusal to submit to blackmail."

"They tackled the wrong fish when they got after me," declared John Amicon on Tuesday at his home on East Rich Street. "I'm not afraid of any man in the United States. I wouldn't give them a cent if it cost my life. They left some dynamite, and I turned it over to the postmaster. My wife found it with a letter demanding $10,000. They never got anything out of me.

"We got a good many letters but turned them over to the post office people as they came in. I understand people in Springfield and Columbus have paid. I couldn't remember the names. Some gave $800, some $1,000. Some fixed it among themselves. They wanted $10,000, but I never paid any attention. They could kill me first."

Rather, a docile prisoner is Sam Lima, alleged leader, who is under arrest at city prison. Lima puffs away at a big black cigar, which parts a heavy mustache and answers questions readily. He is perfectly composed except when "Black Hand" or "Mano Nera," as it is expressed in Italian, is mentioned.

Asked whether or not he had any connection with the Black Hand or other organization similar in nature, Lima jumped to his feet, gesticulating wildly and proclaimed his innocence.

"See, my hands are white. They are not black. I am a hardworking businessman. I work every day, every night, and every Sunday. The Amicons are jealous of me. I sell more bananas than they do. That is why they say I sent the letter. They lie. Bah! No Black Hand. No! No!"

Continuing in a more composed manner after he got that out of his system, Lima said he had been there for three years. He is thirty years old and has a wife and two children. His father and two brothers, all sought by postal authorities, have not been apprehended. Lima says that he and his brothers and father are innocent, and no crime can be fastened upon them.

The men confined at the county jail refuse to be interviewed and have made no statement either denying or admitting the charges. It is this silence, so common among Italians when arrested, that it makes it hard to convict them.

Robert Storaci, probably one of the most highly respected of the Italians in the city expressed no surprise when he learned of the events of the past two days. He knew little of the particulars and expressed the opinion that the authorities must have pretty conclusive evidence since they are making wholesale arrests.

Mr. Storaci says that many of his countrymen are afraid to be prosperous. They are afraid to succeed in business or to accumulate any wealth because of the others of their nationality who desire to live without work and to secure money threatening others. He stated that the laws of the United States and the failure of the courts are largely to blame for the existence of the Black Hand in America. Italians receive these letters, they fear for their lives, and even if they do not give up the money, they hide or burn the letters as they fear they will be killed anyway if the authorities are notified. When they have positive information and secure the conviction of a member or members of any gang for blackmail of this character, the men are only sent to prison for a short term, and they or their friends will have vengeance as soon as the convicted ones are out of prison if not before.

Mr. Storaci suggests that the only method of stamping out the Black Hand in America is by stopping immigration from Italy and by enacting stricter laws, making either life imprisonment or the death penalty in case of conviction.

There is much excitement today in Marion on account of the discovery that the city is a rendezvous for Black Handers. Many Italians quit work for the day and are assembled in groups discussing the happening. It is also claimed that many strangers are in the city and that other members of the gang have come here for the purpose of getting evidence out of the way of the officers.

A statement in yesterday's account of the arrests in the *Mirror* was in error. The existence and operations of the gang were not discovered by tampering with the mail passing between the parties but by the confession of a member of the gang arrested in Pittsburg and by the correspondence captured in the several raids. The laws do not permit the holding up or opening of any mail by government officers except where treason against the government is suspected.

It became known today that the postal authorities were informed of a convention of the Black Hand leaders, which was held here about two months ago, and at that time, it was planned to swoop down upon the crowd and gather them all in. Plans of the Lima store and residence apartments were in the hands of the authorities and about ten officers were detailed to round up the gang.

But after a conference, it was decided that the authorities did not have sufficient evidence to secure convictions, and it was decided to permit the convention to proceed and to gather the crowd in at a later date.

The letters found here are all signed with a drawing of a Black Hand or a heart pierced with a dagger, with drops of blood flowing freely. A skull and cross bones decorate the top of the letters.

And to further illustrate the reach of the "Black Hand," I offer these articles from the *Marion Daily Star* in 1912.

The following story, taken from the *Marion Daily Star* dated Monday, September 23, 1912, is about a murder that took place in a saloon. What interested me was the description of the murder and the mention of the Black Hand.

The headline for our story in capital letters said, "PICKS A QUARREL AND THEN KILLS HIS VICTIM." The second header said, "Shooting in the Saloon of Tony Sylvester Saturday Evening." Then a third header in capital letters said, "ANTONIO FRANCIS SHOT BY ITALIAN." Then in bold print, another lead in to the article, "Italian Witnesses Are Silent as to the Tragedy and Appear To Be Afraid To Talk ¾ Authorities Think Fellow Picks Quarrel With Deliberate Intent to Kill Francis."

Climaxing a bitter quarrel among Italians in the saloon of Tony Sylvester, at Kenton Avenue and Hurr Street, shortly after 5 o'clock Saturday afternoon, an unknown Italian, flashily dressed, shot and instantly killed Antonio Francis, a fellow countryman. With his still smoking revolver clutched in his hand, the slayer rushed out the back door and escaped.

Because of the deep silence maintained by the Italians having knowledge of the shooting and because of their evidences of awful fear of an unseen menace, the authorities are inclined to believe that Francis was a victim of the Black Hand.

Three men accompanied the murderer when he ran through the back door and down the railroad tracks. The authorities have sufficient evidence to lead them to believe that a quarrel was picked with Francis with the deliberate purpose of killing him. No trace of the slayer has been found, and the identity of the three men who accompanied him when he ran from the saloon.

Tony Sylvester, the saloon keeper, says that the slayer was quarrelsome and had been ordered out of the place several times. Each time, however, he would come back. He says he was behind the bar when the shooting occurred, but did not see it. He heard the shots was all, he says.

Giuseppe Laureno, Tony Ventresses, and Giuseppe Martoberieroini saw the shooting, but are unable to throw nay light on the tragedy. "Me don't understand," was about all the authorities got from any of the Italians, when they endeavored to quiz them. No arrests were made. The murdered man was twenty-six years old and came to this country a short time ago. He came to Marion from Toledo three weeks ago and has been working for the Ohio and Western Lime company. He carried a card bearing the address, "No. 4, Superior Street, Toledo, Ohio." Francis was shot through the head with a thirty-eight caliber bullet, his face being badly powder burned. The bullet entered just below the right eye, passed through the brain and lodged just beneath the scalp near the crown of the head.

Two shots were fired by the murderer. Francis evidently struck the slayer's hand at the first shot, the authorities say, and the bullet lodged in the wall. When the second shot was fired, Coroner W. H. Hinklin says the revolver was within a few inches of the victim's face. Uttering an oath in Italian and flourishing his smoking revolver, the unknown slayer and the three men, believed to have been his companions, rushed out and quickly disappeared.

Francis dropped dead near the front of the bar, where his body was found when the coroner arrived.

The Hess & Markert ambulance and the coroner were on the scene before Sheriff John G. Clark or the police were notified of the tragedy. The body was removed to the Hess & Markert undertaking establishment, where the coroner, assisted by Dr. C.G. Smith, held an autopsy.

A search of the dead man's clothing revealed that he had $1.20. He had carried no weapons. One of the Italians, who ran out of the saloon's rear door with the murderer, was called Pete, it was learned by authorities today.

The murderer is described by Tony Sylvester as being rather stockily built, and a sport. He was about twenty-four years old, red-faced and smooth shaven. He wore a brown soft hat and brown clothes. According to Sylvester he made things very disagreeable in his place.

Acting Police Chief A. L. Bond only learned of the shooting when someone asked him about it. He immediately went to the scene, arriving there as the murdered man was being loaded into the ambulance. He made an effort to locate the slayer, but was unable to obtain a clew about his whereabouts.

The funeral service will be held at St. Mary's church, Tuesday morning at 8 o'clock followed by internment in St. Mary's cemetery.

The next article on Tuesday, September 24, 1912, had this headline that said in capital letters, "TONY SYLVESTER SAYS WILL QUIT BUSINESS." The smaller header said, "Will Operate Grocery Instead of a Saloon." And another all-capital-letter header said, "CLAIMS LACKS PROPER POLICE PROTECTION." Then a bold print introduction to the article went on, "Proprietor of Saloon Where Shooting Occurs Complains That He Gives the Police Ample Warning That Trouble Is Imminent—Response Comes Too Late."

Tony Sylvester, in whose saloon in the West End Antonio Francis was killed, Saturday evening, was a caller at the Star office this morning. Sylvester threw some interesting sidelights on the killing, which he asserts was simply the result of a drunken clash.

Sylvester complains that fully eight minutes before the shooting he made an effort to quiet the jangling foreigners, who had become threatening and were out of the control of the proprietor. He telephoned police headquarters that trouble was imminent and wanted an officer, but an officer did not reach the scene of the shooting for a full half hour after the killing, and after the possibility of capturing the murderer, red-handed, had passed.

As to the story that the killing is a development in Black Hand troubles, Sylvester states that it is ridiculous. He states that he and the patrons of his place are too poor to be annoyed by such an organization. Sylvester is positive in his statement that he did not witness the killing. He says his wife and infant child were in the saloon when the trouble arose, and fearing the possibility of a tragedy he assisted them to a room upstairs and called the police. The shots were fired in his absence and the murderer made his escape immediately. (This statement by Tony isn't the same as the one in the previous article. I wonder why his story changed.)

The proprietor of the saloon states that he expects to quit the saloon business and conduct a grocery store. He says the saloon is so located in a dark and disagreeable locality that a business of the kind can not be conducted within the bounds of law and order unless ample police protection is supplied, and it appears impossible to get it.

The funeral services of Francis were held at the St. Mary's church this morning at 8 o'clock. Rev. Father Joseph M. Denning officiated. Interment was made in St. Mary's cemetery.

And so it appears the Black Hand was alive and operating in Marion, even after the arrests and trials of 1909.

CHAPTER 2

The Fated Wedding

The headline of the first newspaper article related indirectly to our
story but seems to fit was found in *The Marion Daily Mirror* newspaper
on June 6, 1911. "Miss Rose Baker Becomes Mrs. Clyde Scranton." Then
the smaller headline goes on to say, "Leave Tomorrow Morning For a

Short Stay in Cleveland and Buffalo After Which They Will Reside in Marion."

Tuesday morning at eight o'clock, a very pretty church wedding was solemnized T St. Mary's church, when Mr. Clyde Scranton and Miss Rose Baker were united in the bonds of matrimony. The ceremony was performed by Rev. Joseph Denning, in the presence of only the immediate family and friends of the contracting parties. Miss Baker, gowned in white and wearing a wedding veil, was attended by Miss Rosella O'Connell. Mr. Albert Steinmetz acted as best man.

Following the ceremony, an elegant wedding breakfast was served at the home of Miss Nettie Pryor, a friend of the bride, on Windsor street. About twenty-five friends and relatives were present at breakfast. The table was prettily decorated with bride roses, with streamers of white ribbon.

Mrs. Scranton is the daughter of Mr. H. P. Baker, of Pearl street., and has occupied a position as night operator at the telephone exchange. The groom is an employee at the Erie transfer. Mr. and Mrs. Scranton leave tomorrow morning for a visit in Cleveland and Buffalo. They will reside in Marion.

And at the time of this happy event, no one could possibly have foreseen the tragedy that was to come to this happy couple.

CHAPTER 3

Murder of Rose Belle

Photo by Mike Perry

Our story, the basis for this document, began on January 29, 1919, but we don't find out until the *Marion Daily Star* hits the newsstand on Thursday, January 30, 1919, with this series of headlines followed by the main story. The large headline starts with "WOMAN'S BODY ON ASH HEAP." The next smaller headline goes on with "Mrs. Clyde Scranton Slain After Attacked." Then we see "FRIGHT IS BELIEVED TO HAVE BROUGHT ON DEATH." Then we see "Evidences of Strangulation and Wound in Forehead." And the last headline says, "Slayer or Slayers

Take Valuables—A West Side Tragedy. Woman Dragged Half Mile. En route Home at Time."

One of the most atrocious crimes that has ever been committed in the city occurred Wednesday night on the West Side when Mrs. Rose Belle Scranton, of No. 265 Cass avenue, was attacked as she neared her home and was later found dead at the coal pile, west of the Erie roundhouse.

The attack was also for robbery and indications are that there were a number of struggles and the victim of the attack put up a desperate battle before death. She had been violated by her assailant or assailants.

Mrs. Scranton, who is the secretary of the National Protective Legion, went to Bucyrus, Wednesday morning, to attend the funeral of Mary Peterman, a sister lodge member, and also to make out papers for the claim. She returned on the car at 8 o'clock in the evening and on her arrival telephoned to her home to have her husband meet her at the corner of Center and Davids street. As Mr. Scranton was attending a meeting at the office of the Erie master mechanic when she phoned, she asked that the porch light be turned on and said she would be home on the next car.

Mrs. L. H. Lessig, a neighbor, who was taking care of the children in the absence of Mr. And Mrs. Scranton, turned on the porch light and was anxiously awaiting Mrs. Scranton's arrival. Mr. Scranton reached home and was somewhat uneasy at his wife not being there. Later he made several trips down the street in search of his wife, until the message came that her body was found.

The first attack on Mrs. Scranton was made at a vacant lot about seventy-five feet from the home of the victim. It was here that her hat, muff, handkerchief, comb and a button off her coat were found, which gave intimation of a struggle at this point. Mrs. Lessig later stated that she remembered hearing a scream shortly before 9 o'clock. She gave no thought of it, however. This was close to the time that Mrs. Scranton would have reached home.

The body of Mrs. Scranton was found by James M. Steel, an inspector at the roundhouse, and Elmer Patten, a fellow workman, on the edge of the coal pile just west of the roundhouse, at 11:15 o'clock. They at once notified Mr. Scranton.

At the time of the finding the body was quite warm, but there were little signs of life. However, the police were notified and medical attention was summoned, but life was extinct.

From the place where the attack was first made to the spot where the body was found is a distance of about a half mile. The body bore a slight scar on the forehead, which barely broke the skin and was only about an inch long about an inch above the nose. The bridge of the nose was skinned and there were two finger nail scratches on the left side of the upper lip. In the absence of Coroner C. L. Baker, Dr. F. V. Murphy was deputized to act. On viewing the remains with other physicians called, he found but a slight mark to indicate that the victim of the assault had been choked and it is thought that she suffered a hart shock from fright as a result of the desperate struggle she had.

The large leather handbag which the victim carried was found a short distance from where the body was found. This contained her gloves, some papers of the insurance lodge to which she belonged, and some articles of a minor nature together with two small pocketbooks. One of these was found aside of the large purse laying open and with the contents gone except a penny which was found near.

The other, which contained two one dollar bills, was in a side compartment of the purse and being flat was overlooked by her assailant. The large handbag was laying near a pole and cross-arm of a telegraph pole was thrown on it. A prayer book, which was apparently new, was found near the body, Mrs. Scranton having been in the habit of carrying it at all times.

Mrs. Scranton, according to her husband, probably had about four dollars when she started on her trip. She wore a diamond ring and a signet ring, a brooch with three small diamonds, a lavalliere set with brilliants and a wrist watch. The brooch was the only piece of jewelry found on her when the body was found.

After the finding of the body the police were at once notified and about all of the men were called into the service on the case. They were assisted by railroad employees and others in an effort to find a clew and run down the guilty party or parties. They worked from the place where the assault was first made to where the corpse was found and this morning the course was gone over several times, but no clew was found.

Five buttons off the victim's coat were found from the place of the attack to where the brutal assailant left his victim, they being scattered along the way.

The long brown coat which Mrs. Scranton wore was covered was covered with burrs and dirt, which with some scratches on her knees, indicated that she had been dragged. The course taken was through the field where the assault was first made and across a corn field to Kenton avenue and hence across where there are signs of the victim having been dragged under a fence and then across a stubble field to where she was found a corpse.

That the victim put up a battle and may have left some marks on her assailant is without much doubt in the minds of those working on the case. The condition of her wearing apparel strongly indicated this fact, while there is no doubt but what her assailant or assailants were engaged in an occupation where they would get very greasy and oily as the clothing and hands of Mrs. Scranton were black with grease.

Following some investigations the officers arrested a colored man who was in an engine cab at the roundhouse. There were a few indications that he might know something about the case, but after being questioned at headquarters his statements were verified to a degree, but he was held temporarily.

Another negro was picked up later, but released this morning. Employees about the roundhouse and in the Erie yards were anxious to find the assailant or assailants this morning, and there is a strong possibility that had he been found he never would have reached the police station.

Mr. Scranton, the husband of the victim, is an engine inspector at the roundhouse and very well known and popular among the employees.

Mrs. Rose Belle Scranton, the victim, would have been twenty-eight years old next August. She was a daughter of H. P. Baker, formerly a photographer of this city, who now resides in the West.

For several years she was chief operator at the Marion County Telephone company's exchange and was very well known in the city and very popular. Her stepmother resides at LaRue. She is also survived by three daughters, Ruth Jeanette, aged four and a half years; Francis Louise, aged two years; and Rita May, aged seven months, together with a sister, Mrs. F. M. Imbody, and a brother who resides in the west.

The *Sandusky Star Journal* reported also on January 30, 1919, on this tragedy, beginning with this headline: "MURDER AT MARION."

> Mrs. Rosa Scranton, 28, wife of Clyde Scranton, Erie railroad inspector, was found dead early today on an ash heap near the Erie roundhouse. Two negroes are being held pending further investigation.

Then on the very next day, January 31, 1919, we find this article with the following headlines: "PROBING INTO WOMAN'S DEATH." "Mrs. Clyde Scranton Dies from Cerebral Blood Clot." "THIS IS REVEALED BY AUTOPSY HELD TODAY." "Police Take Every Precaution To Protect Prisoners." "Irate Railroad Men Prepare To Roast Alive Slayer Had He Been Caught and Identified. Funeral Held Saturday."

> Mrs. Clyde Scranton, of Cass avenue, whose body was found at the edge of a coal pile just north of the Erie roundhouse, late Wednesday night, came to her death as the result of a blood clot on the brain caused by being struck on the head, presumably with a sandbag, in the hands of her unknown assailant. This fact was disclosed by an autopsy performed this morning that revealed a slight bruise and clot of blood under the scalp, the skin not having been broken.
>
> Since the murder of the women the local police, railroad officers and many individuals are working in a effort to fid a clew that will lead to the arrest of the guilty.
>
> Several probable clews were picked up, this morning, near the spot where the woman was attacked within seventy-five feet of her home. These are being held in confidence by the officers in the hope that they may develop some incriminating evidence. Many people have visited the scene of the atrocious crime and the feeling against Mrs. Scranton's assailant is running very high.
>
> Employees in various capacities with the Erie have raised a fund of over $1,000 and are still taking subscriptions with a view to using it to run down the guilty party and a noted detective may be brought to work on the case.
>
> At the same time the local police and railroad detectives are picking up all suspicious looking individuals and there are now colored men being held for investigation, but there is little evidence to fasten the crime on any of them.

Rumor is to the effect that the police received a report in a round about way that a woman was accosted by a tall white man, on north Prospect street, early Wednesday evening, with the motive of robbery but that the woman he grabbed jerked away and ran as the man snarled: "I'll get you yet."

Wednesday evening, a Mexican was said to have been held up and relieved of $30 on Kenton avenue, but this report did not come to the police through the victim.

In the event that the murderer would have been apprehended the morning after the crime and there had been no doubt of his guilt, there is little doubt but that he would have met a terrible end, as the Erie employees were bent on meting out justice and had prepared a fire in an engine in which to punish the assailant.

The police and railroad officials stated this morning that not a stone would be left unturned to bring the guilty party to justice and that clews found this morning may lead to some important developments within the next forty-eight hours.

Authorities are taking every precaution to protect the men under arrest.

The funeral of Mrs. Scranton will be held Saturday morning at 9 o'clock from St. Mary's Catholic church. Rev. Father Joseph M. Denning will officiate. Internment will be made in the St. Mary's cemetery.

After referring to Mrs. Scranton's murder here, following her return home from Bucyrus, the Thursday, January 30, 1919, *Bucyrus Telegraph* says as follows:

Mrs. George J. Willie, of 215 west Galen street, sister of Mrs. Peterman who died suddenly from influenza Tuesday afternoon, states that Mrs. Scranton came to Bucyrus Wednesday morning on the 9 o'clock car for the purpose of identifying the body of Mrs. Peterman, in order that the insurance claim might be proven. Mrs. Scranton is secretary of the National Protective legion of Marion in which the deceased Mrs. Peterman and her husband belonged to the last eight years of her residence there. She had also been in Bucyrus a month ago to identify the body of Ira Peterman, for the same purpose.

She was unable to remain for the funeral of Mrs. Peterman Thursday morning and returned to Marion on the 7 o'clock car Wednesday. She took dinner here at the George Willie home and met quite a number of friends of the deceased Bucyrus woman.

The news that she was murdered soon after she reached her home city after leaving here in full health and evidently without thought of harm to befall her, will shock and grieve deeply the friends she made here.

Mrs. Scranton and the late Ira Peterman and his wife, were rather close friends, all being members of the same fraternal order for years.

Also on January 30, 1919, the *Bucyrus News Forum* reported with this headline and article. "Woman Believed Murdered After Leaving Here Wed" (by United Press) with this dateline:

Marion, January 30—Mrs. Rosa Scranton, twenty-eight, wife of Clyde Scranton, Erie railroad inspector, was found dead early today on an ash heap near the Erie roundhouse. Police say she has been murdered.

Two negroes are being held, pending investigation. An autopsy will be made to determine the cause of her death. The only marks on her body were two bruises above the eyes.

Mrs. Scranton was last seen when she alighted from an interurban car coming from Bucyrus, where she attended a funeral of a friend.

The *Bucyrus Journal* also on Friday, January 31, 1919, reported on Mrs. Scranton's murder with this headline and article: "MURDER AT MARION IS DEPLORED HERE" then "Horror Felt at Death of Mrs. Scranton" and "MISSING CAR IS FATAL." This paragraph then appeared before the article began: "Victim Intended to Leave Bucyrus at 5 p.m. but Was Delayed and Husband Did Not Meet Her as Expected_Caught Within Few Feet of Him and Body Dragged Far."

One of the mst brutal crimes in the history of Marion was that of in which Mrs. Clyde Scranton, secretary of the National Protective League and mother of three small children came to her death within a few hundred feet of her home Wednesday night.

The fact that the murdered woman had been in Bucyrus but an hour before the murder, and that she had met and talked with quite a number of people here, causes an echo here of the horror which is felt in Marion at the manner of her death.

Mrs. Scranton, called here in connection with an insurance claim of Mrs. Ira Peterman, deceased, while here extended an invitation to W. E. Seeger, local secretary of the National Protective Legion, to attend a banquet of the lodge at Marion on Feb. 4th, at which time the grand president and district organiser were to be present. Mr. Seeger had consented to appear on the program, but it is very probable the affair will be cancelled now.

Leaving Bucyrus on a C. M. & B. interurban car at 7 o'clock, Mrs. Scranton reached home before eight, and telephoned from the home of her sister, asking that the porch light at her residence at 265 Cass avenue, be turned on. She learned that her husband could not meet her, though she was nervous about walking home alone, as he was attending a meeting of Erie inspector's at the master mechanic's office.

Mrs. L. B. Lessig, a neighbor, who stayed with the Scranton children while the father was at this meeting, remembers that she heard a faint scream, and one of the Scranton children playing on the floor, also looked up at the sound of what must have been the voice of his murdered mother as she struggled with her assailant.

The finding of a muff, hat, handkerchief, comb and a button off her coat at a vacant lot only 75 feet from her home, showed where the attack on her had taken place. Hours later and a half mile from this point, lying on a coal pile near the Erie roundhouse, the body was found, still warm. Though the woman had been both assaulted and robbed of her money and jewelry, her death is believed to have been caused by heart failure induced by fright, as there were no marks which might have proved fatal. (The next few paragraphs of this article are headed with this intro, "Ghastly Trail is Plain."

A slight scar on the forehead which barely broke the skin, a skinned place on the bridge of the nose and two finger nail scratches on the upper lip were the only marks, about the head, except a slight mark which indicated she may also have been choked.

The heels of her shoes were worn almost completely off and there were scratches on her knees and her clothing was in shreds, indicating she had been dragged to where the body was found.

It is conceded that the victim fought her assailant to the limit of her power. Grease and dirt in quantity on her clothing gave the clue that her assailant was either a mechanic or a laborer employed about machinery, and this clue is counted on heavily to bring the guilty party to justice.

A negro employed at the shops was arrested on suspicion. He seemed to have some proof of his innocence but he is being held for the present.

The dead woman was aged 28 and was formerly chief operator for the Marion County Telephone Co. She had a wide acquaintanceship in Marion and was very popular. She was the daughter of H. P. Baker, formerly a Marion photographer, now located in the west. She is survived by her step-mother, her husband and three daughters; Ruth Jeanette, aged four and a half, Louise, aged two, and Rita May, aged seven. (This is a typo for the News Forum. Rita May was seven months old.)

The fact that Mrs. Scranton missed the five o'clock car out of Bucyrus, which she intended to take was doubtless the deciding circumstance which brought her to her death, as her later arrival prevented her husband meeting her as had been intended.

Then the next day, February 1, 1919, these headlines and story appeared in the *Marion Daily Star*: "MURDER VICTIM BURIED IN ST. MARY'S CEMETERY" followed by "Church Packed at Funeral of Mrs. Clyde Scranton" then "FATHER J. M. DENNING DELIVERS SERMON" and "Authorities Working Hard To Unravel Mystery of Woman's SlayerTwo Clews."

Funeral services for Mrs. Clyde Scranton, who was murdered Wednesday night within seventy-five feet of her home on Cass avenue were held this morning at St. Mary's Catholic church. The large edifice was packed.

Rev. Father Joseph M. Denning conducted the services and preached the sermon. He also conducted the burial service at St. Mary's cemetery.

Father Denning's words were eloquently-touching, and his voice was vibrant with feeling and sympathy.

The pallbearers were J. P. Willauer, J. N. Steel, N. D. Noggle, E. R Ingmair, Charles Stetson and Fred Shroyer.

Among those from a distance who attended the funeral were Mrs. Nora Shark and son Gale, of Kenton; Mr. And Mrs. John Scranton of LaRue; and Mr. And Mrs. Perry Baker and daughter, of Columbus.

Police, railroad detectives and others are continuing their efforts to bring the guilty party or parties to justice.

Every clew is being run down and every suspicious person is being picked up by officers in the hope of apprehending the guilty.

The officers have a couple of clews that may develop some information to warrant an arrest, while the Erie employees in general are assisting in the efforts to capture the assailant or assailants of Mrs. Scranton.

Friday afternoon and evening the officers spent much time searching through cars in the Erie yards for jewelry taken from the woman, but nothing was found.

Only one colored man is now being held at the city prison and there is no evidence to connect him with the crime, but it was hoped that by holding him some of his companions could be apprehended.

Up to this time there have been twelve suspects in the prison.

A dog license on a piece of old belt which had been made into a dog collar, was found near the scene where the woman was attacked and this clew was run down by the police, Friday, but the collar was accounted for, the dog having lost the collar and the owner having secured a duplicate license and a new collar.

Then right next to the preceding article we find this shorter piece of news I'm sure was related to Mrs. Scranton's murder, with this small headline "They Are Dismissed."

Several colored and white fellows who were arrested in the Erie yards Friday evening and locked up on charges of loitering, were turned loose by Mayor Sautter, this morning, without a fine. The men have been employed by the Erie at Kent, and were sent here to draw their money and as a result were compelled to beat their way. They were hanging around the railroad yards waiting to draw their pay when they were taken in charge for loitering, but the mayor considered that the arrests were not warranted and dismissed them.

Chapter 4

Assault Heats Town Up

Activities in Marion as a result of Mrs. Scranton's murder are starting to pick up as we get to the Monday, February 3, 1919, *Marion Daily Star* with these headlines: "NEGRO ATTACKS WHITE WOMAN." Then we have "He is Soon Run Down and Identified" followed by "Later He's Removed to Mansfield Reformatory." And "Ten Marion Men Arrested at Mt. Gilead and Fined—All Saloons Here Closed by Mayor. A Special Grand Jury."

Then after the headlines and before the article, there is a special highlighted bulletin, which has its own headline. "PEOPLE WARNED TO STAY OFF STREETS."

The police department of the city and Sheriff James F. Ullom issued the following statement this afternoon: "Owing to the threatened danger of mob violence, citizens are requested to aid in the enforcement of law by remaining off the streets."

Persons loitering or congregating on the streets will be subject to arrest.

Now the main article begins:

Attempted attack of Margaret Christian, aged about 50 years, wife of A. E. Christian, residing at the junction of Fountain street on Kenton avenue, about 5:25 o'clock Sunday evening, and coming on the heels of the attack and murder of Mrs. Clyde Scranton, last Wednesday night, caused great commotion in the city, Sunday night and early this morning.

Crowds were formed bent on lynching Esquire Warner, known also as George Washington Warner, the colored man arrested for the attempted attack of Mrs. Christian, and he had to be spirited from the city for safety.

The assault on Mrs. Christian occurred just outside the fence of her home as she was returning from making a call on a sick neighbor. Mrs. Christian was hurrying home and after leaving the road she was only a few steps in the yard when she heard someone running back of her. Just as she turned a colored man grabbed her by the throat with his left hand in front and his right on the back of her neck. Mrs. Christian screamed and then gave a second scream when her daughter, Margaret Christian, opened the front door.

At the same time, Miss Mary Dwyer, a neighbor, who happened to be in her yard, heard Mrs. Christian's scream for help and sounded the alarm.

The opening of the door by the daughter of the woman attacked evidently frightened the assailant and he started to run toward the road, tripping over a wire of the fence and falling in the ditch at the side of the road. He arose and ran west to Cottage street and started up the Garden City pike.

News of the attack spread in the neighborhood and William Van Houghton, with a revolver, and Caleb Ballenger started in pursuit of the negro assailant, while Niel Dwyer armed himself with a shotgun and started in the hunt with others. Van Houghton and Ballenger apprehended the alleged assailant at the junction of Lee street and the Garden City pike. They were not long in making him understand that he was their prisoner.

An old straw stack in the field, just north of the Erie roundhouse, is believed by the police to have been the rendezvous of Esquire Warner, the assailant of Mrs. Margaret Christian. When arrested Warner had chaff from oats straw on his back. The police visited the straw pile Sunday evening and again this afternoon and found every indication that men have occupied the place for shelter.

It is also the opinion that the straw stack may have some connection with the man who murdered Mrs. Clyde Scranton last Wednesday night. The straw pile is only about a sixth of a mile beyond where the body of Mrs. Scranton was found. Police have received information that a colored man was seen to go to the straw pile at different times.

The pile was searched to some extent for the jewelry stolen from Mrs. Scranton and by the arrest of Warner another clew is being worked on.

Van Houghton and Ballenger proceeded to march him down Lee street to the West side to turn him over to an officer. A freight train blocked the crossing at Kenton avenue and in order to avoid delay, the men started through the bumpers of the train with their captive, permitting him to go first. When he jumped off he started to run, but Van Houghton was right back of him and under his threat of shooting, the colored man stopped. He was taken to the Werley hotel where he was turned over to Officer Wren, who in turn turned him over to Officer McColly who took him to police headquarters.

At police headquarters the man registered as Esquire Warner. He came from Kentucky about three years ago and is about twenty-two years of age. He has been in the employment of the Erie. His clothes were covered with Spanish needles and burrs of the kind in the ditch where he fell after making the assault. Mrs. Christian was summoned to police headquarters, where she identified Warner as her assailant without hesitation. He denied the accusation, but turned to keep her from getting a good view and to keep from looking her in the face.

As a crowd started to gather about police headquarters and fears of mob violence grew stronger, the police thought it best to take Warner to the county jail. This was done without delay.

Later in the night a crowd of about 200 assembled at police headquarters and all the policemen and deputy sheriffs that could be assembled were called out. After being convinced that Warner was not in the prison, the crowd dispersed, a large portion going to the West Side, where the men threatened to break in the saloon of James Hagan and the officers of the West Side sent for a detail of police to assist them in maintaining order.

After quieting the leaders to a degree, the crowd scattered, and visited sections of the West Side, breaking in the windows of a number of homes of colored families and ordering them to move from the city within twenty-four hours. This was kept up from before midnight until early this morning and colored men on the streets were hissed and warned to leave the city.

Mayor A. J. Sautter was up to 4:30 o'clock this morning to lend assistance in every way to keep Marion's name clean of any mob violence, and acting under advice, ordered all saloons closed for the day. This order was delivered through the officers and was readily complied with.

This morning a large number of colored men waited on the mayor and police to make inquiries regarding the request made on them to leave the city. Many of these were property-owners and have been residents of good standing and reputation and they were advised that there would not likely anything result from the threats and orders made to them, it being the opinion that the men in the crowd are desirous of ridding the city of a certain class that has come from the South during the past two years to do railroad work and do not claim Marion as a place of legal residence.

About 6:30 o'clock last evening after being taken to the county jail by the police officers Sheriff Ullom thought it best to take Warner to Mt. Gilead.

A taxi was secured and Sheriff Ullom took the prisoner to Mt. Gilead, where he was placed in the Morrow county jail. Sheriff Ullom returned to Marion at once and about midnight some 300 came to the local jail and demanded of Sheriff Ullom that he turn Warner over to them.

The crowd was orderly. Sheriff Ullom told the leader that Warner was not in jail and that "if they could find him the man was theirs."

Sheriff Ullom stated that there were too many men in the crowd to let them all in to examine the jail and suggested that a committee of five be named to make the examination. The leader of the men agreed to this proposition and an examination was made. Warner was not found. For a time the crowd was baffled, but word soon leaked out that Warner had been taken to Mt. Gilead.

While the men were examining the jail Judge Grant Mouser called the leader to the telephone and cautioned him not to use violence against Warner and let the law take its course.

Sheriff Ullom said this morning that the men were not in an ugly mood and complied with his requests. Every nook and corner of the jail was examined by the committee of five. Sheriff Ullom even took the men to woman's quarters where there is now a woman prisoner.

This morning about 4:30 o'clock Sheriff Ullom received a call for help from the Mt. Gilead sheriff stating that he was fearful that a mob would take the prisoner away.

In response to the call for help Sheriff Ullom got together two auto loads of men and started for Mt. Gilead. M. C. McNeil took in his car Officers McColley, Shrock, Cusic and Wren, and Chief of Police J. W. Thompson, Sheriff Ullom and W. G. Minshall were driven over by Dan Evans in the latter's car.

When the party arrived at Mt. Gilead it found that Warner had been removed to some other jail. It was learned this morning that Warner had been taken to the Mansfield reformatory.

Judge Grant Mouser announced this morning that a special session of the grand jury would be called within the next two days to take up Warner's case. Judge Mouser stated that justice would be as speedy as possible and in a consultation with members of last night's crowd made it explicit that no time would be lost in trying Warner. Judge Mouser sent a letter to Judge Calvin H. Wood, of Mt. Gilead, this morning, that the men held at Mt. Gilead be released as soon as possible.

Judge Mouser stated this morning that the grand jury would in all possibility be asked to investigate conditions on the West Side with a view to a clean up.

A federal detective arrived in Marion this morning to investigate conditions on the West Side and to assist the local officers in apprehending the murderer of Mrs. Scranton.

The next item from Mt. Gilead following the above article had this headline. "Story from Mt. Gilead"

Mt. Gilead, Ohio, February 3. (Special.)

Ten Marion men were arraigned in the mayor's court here this morning following their visit to the Morrow county jail this morning at 3 o'clock in connection with the arrest of Warner.

The men, giving their names as E. C Northup, C. W. Brickley, H. C. Osborne, T. Trell, W. E. Finch, W. V. Towers, E. E. Towers, W. F. Lindsey, O. H. Monts and Will Christian, each were fined twenty-five dollars and costs, which amounted in all to $29.33.

One of the men wore a sailor's suit, another wore a soldiers uniform with overseas service stripes.

Warner was brought to Mt. Gilead about 10 o'clock last night and placed in jail for safekeeping. About 3 o'clock this morning five men stopped at a residence across the street from the jail and asked to be directed to that institution. Reaching the jail, the party, which had been enlarged to twelve, aroused Sheriff John Vanatta.

The men told the sheriff they would like to be taken through the jail. He informed them that he was not in the habit of taking visitors through the jail at that hour and told them to come back later.

After the men were gone the Sheriff notified Deputy Sheriff Ned Russell and enough men to protect the jail were deputized. When the Marion men again made their appearance they were immediately placed under arrest and confined in the insane ward.

Deputy Sheriff Russell then got his auto, hurried the prisoner into it and rushed him out of Morrow county.

The Marion party had intended upon making sure that Warner was in the jail at Mt. Gilead, to notify others in Marion, but were apprehended before they could do so. The men came in three autos, one having been parked in front of the courthouse, one back of that building and another on the square.

Then right below this news from Mt. Gilead was this announcement by the county commissioners with this headline "$1,000 reward for murderer of woman."

Then this smaller headline "It is Offered by County Commissioners Today."

A reward of $1,000 for the arrest and conviction of the murderer or murderers of Mrs. Clyde Scranton was offered by the board of county commissioners this afternoon.

In offering the reward the commissioners stated that if more than one are implicated and convicted only $1,000 will be given the man who makes the arrest or apprehends the criminals.

The *Bucyrus News Forum* had this item on February 4, 1919, with this headline: "MARION MOB FOLLOWS POSSE TO MT. GILEAD."

(By United Press) Marion, February 3:

> George Washington Warner, a negro, who was taken into custody charged with assaulting Mrs. Margaret Christian on the street near her home Saturday night, has been removed to the Mansfield courthouse for safekeeping.
>
> A mob attacked the jail here and demanded of Sheriff James Ullom the delivery of the prisoner, but the sheriff eluded the some 300 enraged people and had the prisoner removed first to Mt. Gilead to keep him from the mob.
>
> A part of the mob, however, in autos followed to Mt. Gilead, where they demanded of Sheriff Wayland of Morrow county the delivery of Warner. Wayland had prepared for the emergency and had a dozen sworn deputies on hand and put 10 of the mob under arrest. The other lost nerve and fled.
>
> In order to be still more safe, Wayland and Ullom then arranged to have Warner taken to Mansfield.
>
> All saloons in Marion have been ordered closed, and the police have been ordered to prohibit any congregating on the streets.

CHAPTER 5

Beginning of Racial Discord

The *Marion Daily Star* on Tuesday, February 4, 1919, continues the story of the impact of Mrs. Scranton's murder and the assault on Mrs. Christian with this headline: "QUIET NIGHT FOLLOWS TROUBLE MONDAY," then this smaller headline, "More Than 200 Negroes Leave the City" followed by this headline, "PROSECUTOR INTERVIEWS PRISONER AT MANSFIELD." And the last headline of this article is "Saloons Are Reopened_Windows Broken in Colored Peoples Homes."

Following a night and day of threatened trouble due to the attempted attack of Mrs. A. E. Christian, Sunday afternoon, and the brutal murder of Mrs. Clyde Scranton, Wednesday night, which aroused the ire of railroad employees and many other citizens against Esquire Warner, alias George Washington Warner, arrested for attempting to attack Mrs. Christian, things were very quiet in the city Monday night.

To guard against a possible outbreak, outside police assistance was summoned and in response to the call for police protection, Captain Billington, of the Big Four police department, and Captain Moran, of the Erie police department, placed to the service of the city their entire forces which consisted of twenty-five men, while some special men were furnished by the Hocking Valley and Pennsylvania departments.

Chief J. W. Thompson had the entire force of the local police department in service and, with the deputies secured by Sheriff J. F. Ullom, there were in all about 150 men who were armed to preserve order. This force will be maintained to as large a degree as possible to lend protection to life and property.

The absence of negroes from the city was very noticeable today. Signs posted on the West Side, Monday morning, ordering the colored population to move, bore this inscription:

"T.N.T._Travel Nigger Travel."

This seemed to have brought the desired result, as it is estimated that over 200 colored people left the city before daylight this morning. Approximately 100 men were paid off and discharged from the service of the Erie, these having been employed mostly at the roundhouse and transfer station. Some of these were so scared that they feared going after their pay and still have their checks.

With most negroes, it was simply a desire to get out of the city, and they were not particular in which direction they went, taking the first train that was convenient.

The union station was well filled with colored men and a number of women. Monday evening, most of these were taking the Hocking Valley train for Columbus. According to a special from Columbus, this morning, over 100 arrived there and many spent the night in the depot. The interurban car leaving here at 5:15 Monday afternoon carried twenty-one colored passengers, while every car and train out of Marion, Monday, carried some.

After the Hocking Valley train left Monday evening, four colored men were all that were in the depot. Three of these went to the ticket window and purchased tickets for Bellefontaine. When the fourth walked up close behind the others, the ticket clerk asked him if he wanted a ticket to Bellefontaine. The colored man replied: "No, boss, dat 'aint fah nuff. Gib me one to Indianapolis." He was accommodated and demonstrated a feeling of unrest until the train started out of the city.

Employees of the waterworks and gas companies had a busy time, Monday afternoon, reading and taking out meters on the West Side. Some of the residents who left did not stop to pack their furniture, trusting that their landlords would look after this for them, while those who only had a suitcase to pack were the first to get away.

Many of the houses that were occupied by colored families have all the windows broken out and what colored inhabitants

Marion has that have been residents and considered citizens are keeping off the streets for the time to avoid any outbreak.

One saloon-keeper on the West Side stated this morning that he might as well discontinue business, as the colored men employed by the Erie constituted practically all of his trade. Several close observing persons remarked at noon, today, that they had not seen a colored person on the streets this morning.

Up to this afternoon, no charge had been filed against Warner, the assailant of Mrs. Christian. As Warner will have to be arraigned and tried here, he will be brought here secretly from Mansfield and given a chance to plead so as to arouse as little excitement as possible. No fear of any violence is anticipated by the police or officials and this morning Mayor A. J. Sautter rescinded the order closing the saloons.

The local police are still making an effort to get a trace of the jewelry stolen from Mrs. Clyde Scranton the night she was murdered. It is thought that the murderer would peddle this to individuals rather than take it to a store or pawn shop and that by giving the matter publicity some of it may be brought to light with a description of the man who sold it. This is practically the only hope of the police in securing information that may result in the guilty party or parties being apprehended.

Prosecuting Attorney Hector S. Young went to Mansfield this afternoon and will try and secure a confession from Warner regarding the murder of Mrs. Clyde Scranton.

Local officers are of the opinion that Warner may be able to throw some light on the party or parties who killed Mrs. Scranton.

George Washington Warner, a negro, identified as the assailant of a Marion woman, is in the Richland county jail for safekeeping, having been taken from Marion to Mt. Gilead to escape violence and later being spirited here from that village after plans had been made to go to Mt. Gilead after him, says Monday's Mansfield News.

Warner was brought here in an automobile this morning by Sheriff John Vanatta, former Sheriff Charles Chilcote and Deputy Sheriff E. B. Russell, of Morrow county. They arrived at 7 o'clock and five minutes later Warner, apparently unconcerned was

engaged in a game of checkers at the county jail, where he had
been placed in charge of Sheriff Kaufman.

No information is available as to the length of time Warner
will be held here, but in all probability be until conditions have
quieted down sufficiently in Marion to make it safe to return there
for trial. While it is not anticipated that any steps will be taken
to secure Warner now that he is in the Richland county jail. All
necessary precautions will be taken by Sheriff Kaufman to protect
the prisoner while he is in custody in this city.

CHAPTER 6

Exodus from Marion

The news in Marion was being reported in other cities. The *Lima Daily News* on February 3, 1919, had an item with this headline: "MOB FOILED IN HANGING NEGRO." Then a smaller headline said, "Man Held For Attack on Woman In Marion Is Taken To Mansfield."

Dateline Marion:

George Washington Warner, colored, arrested Sunday for attacking Mrs. Margaret Christian on the street near her home, was removed to the county jail at Mansfield Monday, following an unsuccessful attempt by a mob of 300 to lynch him at he jail here and at Mt. Gilead.

Foiled in their attempt to secure the surrender of Warner by Sheriff James F. Ullom, who had Warner removed to Mt. Gilead for safekeeping, part of the mob went to Mt. Gilead in automobiles and demanded Sheriff Wayland of Morrow county to turn over Warner to them. Instead, Wayland summoned 12 deputies and placed 10 members of the mob under arrest. The rest fled.

Fearing further trouble here, all saloons were ordered closed Monday and police were ordered to permit no congregating in the streets. Several loiterers were arrested.

The Sandusky Star Journal also reported on February 3, 1919 this news with this headline. "averts lynching; mob is 'pinched'." The smaller headline says Mt. Gilead Sheriff Dampens Ardor of Marion Citizens After Negro."

George Washington Warner, colored, arrested yesterday for attacking Mrs. Margaret Christian on the street near her home, was removed to the county jail at Mansfield today following an unsuccessful attempt by a mob of 300 to lynch him at the jail here and at Mt. Gilead.

Foiled in their attempt to secure the surrender of Warner here by Sheriff James F. Ullom, who had Warner removed to Mt. Gilead for safekeeping, part of the mob went to Mt. Gilead in automobiles and demanded Sheriff Wayland of Morrow county to turn Warner over to them. Instead Wayland summoned twelve deputies and placed ten members of the mob under arrest. The rest fled.

Fearing further trouble here, all saloons were ordered closed today and police were ordered to permit no congregating in the streets. Several loiterers were arrested.

On February 4, 1919, *The Hamilton Daily Republican News* reported on Marion with an article and this headline: "MOB IN MARION TRIES TO LYNCH NEGRO IN JAIL." The smaller headline said, "Attack on Aged Woman Stirs Ohio City—Mexican also Suspected."

Orders against assemblies on the streets and warnings to negroes to leave the city were issued today following an attack upon Mrs. Margaret Christian, 50.

A negro, George W. Warner, 20, is under arrest. A crowd of 300 visited the jail and demanded Warner's custody, but the prisoner had been spirited away.

Warner was identified by Mrs. Christian as having attacked her at her home on Fountain street late Sunday afternoon. Mrs. Christian was attacked a short distance from where Mrs. Clyde Scranton was murdered last Wednesday night.

A Mexican was arrested as a suspect and is thought to have threatened two girls going home from church Sunday night. Both men were secretly removed to another town when a portion of the mob followed to Mt. Gilead.

From Mt. Gilead the two prisoners are said to have been taken to Mansfield.

In the Sandusky Star-Journal datelined Marion, O, Feb. 4 (1919) an article appeared with this headline. "Marion Negroes In Fear of Lynching Leave; City Quiet."

The southern negro colony in the Erie railroad yards was deserted today. Over 200 left the city last night after warnings had been posted at the Erie roundhouse following the attack Sunday upon Mrs. Margaret Christian and the subsequent efforts to lynch her alleged assailant, George Warner, who was spirited first to the Morrow county jail and later to the reformatory at Mansfield.

No further trouble is expected.

Mayor Sautter expected to permit saloons to reopen today.

Then Marion's news appeared in the El Paso, Texas, *Herald* also on February 4, 1919, with this headline: "NEGROES RUN OUT OF TOWN."

With the dateline Marion, Ohio, February 4:

An exodus of negroes was in progress here following the postings of warnings ordering them to leave the city by 6 o'clock last night. The few remaining were in their homes behind barred doors, as trouble was feared.

The warnings resulted from an attack upon Mrs. Margaret Christian, near where Mrs. Clyde Scranton was murdered Wednesday night.

And from the *Sandusky Register* on Tuesday, February 4, 1919, we find this headline with this article: "NEGROES FLEE FROM MARION WHEN FEELING OVER MURDER WHITE WOMAN RUNS VERY HIGH."

Datelined Marion, Ohio, February 3:

An exodus of negroes from this city was in progress here today, following the posting of warnings ordering them to leave the city by 5 o'clock tonight. The few still here were in their homes behind barred doors tonight.

The warnings were posted following the attack yesterday upon Mrs. Margaret Christian where Mrs. Clyde Scranton was attacked and slain, presumably by a negro, late Wednesday night.

Although George W. Warner, the negro accused of the attack upon Mrs. Christian, is in Mansfield reformatory tonight following threats of lynching early today, feeling runs high.

The business district was placarded with orders from the
mayor and the sheriff, forbidding loitering and congregating. It
was observed in the downtown streets tonight, but it was reported
that a large crowd of men had congregated on the West Side, and,
despite the fact that saloons have been closed by order of the
mayor, many in the crown were reported to have been drinking.

Judge Grant C. Mouser of the common pleas court announced
today that a special session of the grand jury would be called soon
to consider Warner's case.

The next article in the *Marion Daily Star* comes the very next day
from the above item on Wednesday, February 5, 1919, with this set
of headlines: "HE JUST WANTED TO PUT HIS ARMS AROUND HER" then this,
"Case of Mistaken Identity, Warner Tells Prosecutor" followed by
"WHO INTERVIEWS HIM IN JAIL AT MANSFIELD" and "Negroes Too Scared
To Return to Marion, Authorities Say. Not Wanted at Galion."

"I admit I put my arms around Mrs. Margaret Christian last
Sunday night, but I did not know it was her and thought it was a
friend of mine," said Esquire Warner, alias George Washington
Warner, to Prosecuting Attorney Hector S. Young, yesterday
afternoon in the Richland county jail at Mansfield, according to
the Marion county prosecutor.

Prosecuting Attorney Young and Police Captain A. L. Bond
went to Mansfield yesterday to question Warner and find out, if
possible, if he was implicated in the brutal murder of Mrs. Clyde
Scranton, Wednesday night, January 29.

Warner told the officers that he mistook Mrs. Christian for a
friend of his and just stopped to talk to her regarding a matter. He
stated he had no motive of robbery or attack.

Warner told the officers that he was in Galion the night before
the Scranton murder and in Crestline the night of the murder. He
gave the officers a number of names of men who were with him on
these two nights and officers today are attempting to corroborate
Warner's statements.

No charge has yet been placed against Warner. Officers are
attempting to secure further evidence before having Mrs. Christian
file an affidavit.

Authorities do not believe that negroes who have fled Marion can be induced to return here to go to work again, even though their employers sought to have them come back. The majority of them, particularly those from the South, were greatly frightened and there is little chance of any of them coming back, according to authorities.

The *Bucyrus Union Telegraph* yesterday all: (was in the *Marion Daily Star*)

Seven trunks belonging to Marion colored folks who had fled the city, were at the C., & M. B. Freight Depot here last night, and their owners are said to have been harbored over night in one of the Aumiller building.

The *Galion Enquirer* yesterday carried the following:

Negroes ordered out of Marion are not wanted here, and will be given quick orders to move on.

Last night a number of colored fellows from Marion, got off Big Four train, 10, and hung around the depot. The railroad authorities gave them to understand that they must move, and as there was plenty of money in the crowd they purchased tickets and went east on No. 26.

There has been no recent disturbance on part of the colored people of this city, but police authorities are keeping watch over them.

CHAPTER 7

Labor Changes

Then on February 7, 1919, in the *Marion Daily Star*, we find this notice, an event, while not part of the murder of Mrs. Scranton or the assault on Mrs. Christian certainly is a consequence of the reaction perpetrated by the lynch mobs and their "TNT" activities. This article in the *Star* had this headline: "WHITE LABOR REPLACES NEGRO LABOR ON ERIE," followed by this smaller headline, "Company Is Not Suffering for Lack of Help" and by "THIS ANNOUNCEMENT IS GIVEN OUT TODAY." Then "About 100 Negroes Formerly Employed by Erie Discharged."

> Although about 100 Southern negro employees of the Erie were discharged within the past week, the company is not suffering for want of help. Only a small number of the men were employed at the transfer and their places have been filled so far as necessary to handle the work. Some were employed on the section, while the majority were doing duty about the roundhouse.
>
> White labor has replaced the men and their services are only missed by the conspicuousness of their absence, it was announced today.

CHAPTER 8

George Washington Warner

Our next article comes from the *Marion Daily Star* on Thursday, February 6, 1919, with this headline: "ALIBI AS ADVANCED BY COLORED SUSPECT" with a smaller headline, "Mansfield Paper's Version of Prosecutor's Visit There."

What is regarded as a good alibi in the murder of Mrs. Clyde Scranton, at Marion last Wednesday evening, was established by George Washington Warner, negro suspect, when he was questioned late yesterday afternoon by Prosecuting Attorney Hector Young and a police official at Marion, at the Richland county jail where the suspect is being held, says Wednesday's Mansfield News.

The Marion officials arrived in this city yesterday at 4:30 p. m. and grilled Warner for an hour. They were trying to connect him with the murder of Mrs. Scranton, as well as the alleged assault upon Mrs. Margaret Christian, Sunday evening, at her home in the west part of Marion.

Warner, who is also known as Squires, told the Marion officials he was in Galion the night before Mrs. Scranton was murdered and gave the names of two men he claims he was with. The prosecutor took the names of these men and went from here to those towns to verify the story of Warner.

Warner admits he saw Mrs. Christian as she was passing along the street in Marion and says he looked at her but denies that he laid hands on her. Mrs. Christian claims he choked her. The negro says he was drunk Sunday afternoon. Sheriff Kaufman corroborates this statement by saying that liquor could be smelled on Warner's breath when he was brought to this city early Monday morning to get him away from a mob that thought it wanted to lynch him.

Assault and battery is now the strongest charge that officials now believe they can place against Warner. The Marion officials are still at sea over the brutal murder of Mrs. Scranton, although her body was found forty-five minutes after the murder.

Then the *Marion Daily Star* on Wednesday, February 12, 1919, had this article with these four headlines: "SPECIAL GRAND JURY TO CONSIDER WARNER CASE" then a smaller "Negro Charged with Attempting to Attack White Woman" followed by "Sherman Peck's Wife Says He's Bad Actor" and followed by "Knocks Out Her Teeth and Pulls Her Hair Out by Handsful, She Says."

Prosecuting attorney Hector S. Young today called a special session of the grand jury for tomorrow at 9 o'clock following a conference with Judge Grant E. Mouser.

The grand jurors will consider the case of Esque Warner, colored, nineteen years old, alias George Washington Warner, charged with attempting to attack Mrs. Margaret Christian, wife of A. E. Christian, late Sunday afternoon, February 2.

The grand jury for this term of court has not been dismissed and no special venire will be necessary.

Judge Mouser announced this morning that Warner's trial will be made as speedy as possible and that it will be set immediately following Warner's indictment.

The *Marion Daily Star* has our next article on Wednesday, February 12, 1919, with these headlines: "WARNER ARRAIGNED HERE AND HURRIED AWAY AGAIN" followed by "Preliminary Hearing Held in County Jail Late Tuesday" then "JUSTICE HABERMAN FIXES WARNER'S BOND AT $5,000" and "Negro Admits He Hears of the Scranton Murder in Crestline Night Woman Is Slain."

Esque Warner, colored, alias George Washington Warner, was hurried to Marion late yesterday from the Richland county jail at Mansfield and arraigned before Justice Charles W. Haberman in the county jail on a charge of attempted attack. Justice Haberman found sufficient evidence to bind Warner over to the Grand Jury under bond of $5,000. Warner is charged with attempting to attack Mrs. Margaret Christian, wife of A. E. Christian, in her door-yard the late afternoon of February 2.

Warner was later captured and after being lodged in the county jail, he was later rushed ti Mt. Gilead and from there to Mansfield for safe keeping.

When arraigned, yesterday afternoon, Warner admitted he intended to attack Mrs. Christian. The hearing was held secretly in the county jail. The only persons present at the hearing were sheriff James Ullom, Prosecuting Attorney Hector S. Young, Police Chief J. W. Thompson and newspapermen.

Immediately following the hearing Warner was hurried out of town and will be kept "somewhere in Ohio" until he is brought back to Marion for trial, it is announced.

Officers are leaning to the opinion that Warner knows more than he is telling about the murder of Mrs. Clyde Scranton Wednesday night January 29.

When quizzed by officers yesterday afternoon Warner had alibis for Tuesday evening and Thursday evening, but made several statements about his whereabouts Wednesday evening.

In closely questioning Warner he told officers that he learned of the Scranton murder Wednesday night at Crestline.

Warner said that he arrived in Crestline Wednesday and went to one of the Negro shanties. He said that in the course of a conversation with a man named Luci he was told that a murder had been committed at Marion and that all Negroes had been forced to leave the city. Warner told officers he thought nothing more of it and came back to Marion Thursday morning by way of Bucyrus.

Local officers point to the fact that Warner, when arrested Sunday night following the Christian attack, had straw on his clothing, but Warner denies being at the strawstack near the Christian home. They also point to the fact that the direction taken by the slayer or slayers of Mrs. Scranton was toward the strawstack. This leads officers to the opinion that Warner lived in the strawstack but he stoutly denied this yesterday.

Warner's stories are being investigated by the officers as well as his movements Tuesday, Wednesday and Thursday evenings.

Our next article comes from the *Sandusky Register* on Wednesday, February 12, 1919, with this dateline, Marion, Ohio, February 11, and this headline: "Colored Assailant Brought To Marion."

> George Washington Warner, colored, who was held at Mansfield, following an alleged assault on Mrs. Margaret Christian here February 2, was returned here today for preliminary trial. Justice C. W. Haberman bound him over to the grand jury under $5,000 bond. He was taken to a neighboring city for safe keeping.
>
> Warner has been exonerated from implication in the murder of Mrs. Rose Scranton which occurred shortly before his alleged assault upon Mrs. Christian. The two crimes caused a near race riot in this city, causing an exodus of most of the colored population of Marion.

On Thursday, February 13, 1919, the *Sandusky Star Journal* had this headline with this item datelined Marion, Ohio, February 13: "GOES TO MANSFIELD."

> Three hours after he was indicted on a charge of attempting to attack Mrs. Margaret Christian, Esque Warner, alias George Washington Warner, was on his way to Mansfield today to serve an indeterminate sentence in the state reformatory. Attempts were made to lynch Warner February 2, but he was spirited out of town.

And the above same news item was reported in the *Lima Daily News* also on February 13, 1919, word for word.

The *Bucyrus News Forum* had this item on Friday, February 14, 1919, with a very large headline: "MARION NEGRO SAVED FROM MOB IS SENT TO STATE REFORMATORY."

(By United Press) Marion, February 13:

> Three hours after his indictment here today Esque Warner, alias George Washington Warner, colored, charged with having assaulted Mrs. Margaret Christian, was on his way to the Mansfield Reformatory to serve an indeterminate sentence.
>
> An attempt was made to lynch Warner here on February 2nd.
>
> The authorities, however, spirited the captive out of town.

CHAPTER 9

Isaac Hill

The murder investigation takes another turn as we look at the *Marion Daily Star* on March 7, 1919, with this headline in half-inch bold print letters: "ISAAC HILL; NEGRO, SAYS HE AND ESQUE WARNER MURDER MRS. CLYDE SCRANTON." The next, smaller headline says, "Hill Makes Confession, Telling of Crime in Detail," which is followed by this headline: "HE SAYS THEY DID NOT INTEND TO KILL HER" then "Hill Confesses After He's Arrested by Sheriff" followed by "Identifies Warner in Reformatory at Mansfield Yesterday. Hill Mental DefectiveBrutal Crime of January 29."

After various clews for the past thirty days, Sheriff James F. Ullom made an arrest Monday morning that he believes will lead to the solution of the murder of Mrs. Clyde Scranton, the night of January 29. News of the arrest has been suppressed at the request of the authorities.

The arrest was made by Sheriff Ullom, assisted by Deputies James I. Morton and W. L. Morral, along the tracks of the Pennsylvania railroad in Pleasant Township.

Sheriff Ullom has now in custody a negro, Isaac Hill, about 36 years of age. Hill has made a confession. Authorities say he is a mental defect.

Monday morning Sheriff Ullom received a call from Pleasant township stating that a negro was wandering about the country frightening women in the township and making threats against men.

Sheriff Ullom called a taxi and together with W. L. Morral hurried to Pleasant township. When they arrived in the township, it was found that the negro was gone and all trace of him was lost. Deputy Morton started in another machine in search of the negro, but was unable to find any clew.

The same morning about 10 o'clock Sheriff Ullom saw a negro walking down the tracks of the Pennsylvania railroad. He went to the negro and placed him under arrest. At the time Hill was walking north toward Marion.

When Sheriff Ullom placed Hill under arrest he said to him : "Don't you know that this is a bad place for negroes to come?"

Hill then started voluntarily to give a detailed description of the Scranton murder. The officers at once drew him out and learned he knew every detail of the crime.

Hill was brought to Marion and placed in county jail, but the officers made no announcement of the arrest until today. The officers went on the theory that Hill could not be telling the truth, as his story was too preposterous, they said. And it was told in such a disconnected manner. But, when Hill, time and time again, stated that he helped commit the crime the officers commenced an investigation of his actions.

Here is the story Hill told Prosecuting Attorney Hector S. Young:

"I worked at the plant of the Commercial Steel Castings company. Two days after I quit there I met 'Baby Face,' at Dora Harper's late in the afternoon and from there we went to Jimmie Hagan's saloon. When we come out of there we saw a woman going along a sidewalk and followed her

"She turned across a path and I and 'Baby Face' accosted her she screamed and 'Baby Face' grabbed her. From the struggle she became weak and exhausted and could not do much.

"We took her across lots and under two board fences. We took her through a field to the coal pile. Here she regained consciousness and screamed. 'Baby Face' picked up a stick and hit her over the head with a stick.

"We saw lanterns in the field and then we took out. The next day I went to the plant and drew my money and left town."

Officers pointed out that "Baby Face" to whom Hill referred was Esque Warner. The officers also state that the murder of Mrs.

Scranton was not committed until January 29, while Hill claims it was two after he was discharged from the plant of the Commercial Steel Castings company. Hill was discharged December 4, according to testimony given Prosecutor Young. The pawn ticket found on Hill showed that it was pawned December 25.

Prosecutor Young points out that Hill is of low mentality and has no conception of time or dates.

Prosecutor Young stated this morning that on Hill's person was found a hospital discharge certificate from a hospital in Portsmouth. The slip also states that he was in the hospital but two days, which Hill claims is true. Officers think that possibly there might have been a mistake in the date of the hospital and that Hill might have entered it at a later date.

If Hill was admitted into the hospital January 30, officers are of the opinion that Hill has no connection with the Scranton murder. Hill, the slip states, was working for the N. & W. Railroad at the time he was admitted to the hospital.

This part of the story is being investigated by the officers in an effort to find just when Hill entered the hospital and when he worked for the N. & W. Railroad.

Hill's recital of the details was so accurate in most details, according to the officers, that Hill was taken to the scene of the murder to see if he could point out the route taken or if he had simply imagined it.

Hill went over every detail of the crime from the place where Mrs. Scranton was attacked to the place where she was found. Officers state that Hill showed them where he and Warner took Mrs. Scranton under a fence and over two other fences. Every little detail of the crime was complete in Hill's mind and he did not hesitate once when going over he ground.

Sheriff Ullom points out how the body was thrown over two fences and under another, which is what actually happened according to the officers.

Hill told the officers that after the murder he left for Bucyrus and "Baby Face" went to Galion. This part of the story is corroborated by Warner's actions, officers say. At the time Warner was arrested and convicted on his own plea of guilty of attempting to attack Mrs. Margaret Christian a few nights after the Scranton murder.

Hill at times seems demented, then again he is perfectly rational, officers say. The murder seems to prey on his mind, according to officers, and he apparently is laboring under a great strain.

Hill says they did not intend to kill Mrs. Scranton.

When asked by officers what became of the signet ring, which was missing when Mrs. Scranton was found the night of the murder, Hill stated that he had sold it at Portsmouth. He could not tell the name of the person to whom it was sold, but he was sure he sold it at Portsmouth. Officers are investigating this story.

Officers say that Hill is too ignorant to have imagined the details of the murder and could not have given such a vivid description if he were not implicated in it.

When Prosecutor Young asked Hill why he had come to Marion, Hill said he could not sleep and had been wandering about the country and something seemed to force him to come back here. Prosecutor Young states that this is the history of many murderersthey always return to the scene of the crime.

When Warner, who is nineteen, was arraigned in court following his attack on Mrs. Christian, aged about fifty, he stoutly denied any connection with the Scranton murder. At the time local officers believed he knew more than he was telling.

When Warner was given a preliminary hearing before Justice Charles W. Haberman in the county jail, he told the officers that the first time he heard of the Scranton murder was Wednesday night at Galion through a negro. The Scranton murder was committed Wednesday night and officers, at the time were suspicious of Warner's actions, but Warner's statements could not be refuted.

When Hill was arrested Sheriff Ullom knew nothing of his connection with the murder and it was only by mere chance that he was taken into custody.

Yesterday Prosecuting Attorney Young and Sheriff Ullom with a number of deputies took Hill to the Mansfield reformatory to see if he could identify Warner.

A line of seven negroes was placed in a room at the institution, among them Warner. Hill was then brought in and asked by the officers to pont out the man he had been talking about.

Hill without hesitating walked over to Warner. Warner stood up and shook hands with Hill. Warner was then confronted with Hill's story, which he stoutly denied.

The officers kept telling Warner, "You are smart and Hill is ignorant," in an effort to break Warner down, but all attempts were unsuccessful, according to the officers.

Once Warner jumped to his feet and grabbing a chair, started to assault Hill. He was stopped before he could reach Hill.

Wednesday afternoon at the county jail sheriff Ullom showed Hill a picture of Warner and Hill said when asked who it was, "Why, that is 'Baby Face!' "

Hill says that following the murder Warner gave him five dollars and a signet ring. The remainder of the jewelry taken from Mrs. Scranton was kept by Warner. Three rings and a wrist watch were taken from Mrs. Scranton at the time of the murder, officers say.

Hill says that Warner did all the work and he only did what Warner told him to do.

Hill was left at the Mansfield reformatory in order that the officials at the reformatory may use him to get a confession from Warner. Warner will be given a grilling today in an effort to extort a confession from him.

Officers said this morning that they did not wish to fasten the murder on Warner and Hill if it is not established beyond a reasonable doubt that Hill is telling the truth. They are carefully investigating all of Hill's story, especially the hospital certificate from Portsmouth. Hill is said by officers to be a mental enigma.

At the time of the murder the board of county commissioners offered a reward of $1,000 for the arrest and conviction of the murderer or murderers of Mrs. Scranton.

Under the law Sheriff Ullom, in the event of conviction, will not receive the reward, as it is provided that no officer may receive any reward for the arrest and conviction of a criminal.

On March 8, 1919, the story continues with this article and these headlines: "CORROBORATING FACTS SOUGHT IN CONFESSION," followed by "Authorities Checking up Statements Made by Hill" then by "WHO SAYS HE HELPS TO KILL MRS. CLYDE SCRANTON" and by "Negro Persists in Telling Same Story of Brutal Crime Over and Over."

Prosecuting Attorney Hector S. Young and Sheriff James F. Ullom were busily engaged today seeking evidence to corroborate the confession of Isaac Hill of the murder of Mrs. Clyde

Scranton January 29. Hill confessed to the crime implicating Esque Warner, who is now serving a sentence in the Mansfield reformatory for attacking Mrs. Margaret Christian a few nights after the murder.

The officers are seeking confirmation of many of Hill's statements regarding the murder. The Portsmouth officers have been called into the case in an effort to find out when Hill arrived in Portsmouth and when he was taken to a hospital there.

Hill in his confession said that he was in a hospital at Portsmouth. When arrested he had on his person a hospital discharge slip showing he had been admitted into the institution January 30 and discharged February 2. The two officers are endeavoring to find out if the dates on the slip are correct. There is some disposition on the part of the officers to believe that a mistake has been made by hospital authorities.

Officers hinted this morning some new developments might be made Monday in the case, but refused to give any information further on the matter.

Officers stated this morning that Hill went over the story a number of times yesterday and every time told it the same. Officers say that Hill has told exactly the same story since he was arrested Monday morning in Pleasant township by Sheriff Ullom and Deputy Sheriff W. L. Morral.

As part of the follow-up of the above stories, we have this next article from the March 11, 1919, *Marion Daily Star* with this headline: "PROSECUTOR AND SHERIFF AT PORTSMOUTH TODAY," followed by this smaller headline, "Seek Corroborative Evidence in Hill's Murder Confession."

Prosecuting Attorney Hector S. Young and Sheriff James F. Ullom left today for Portsmouth where they will make an investigation of the story of Isaac Hill, who made an alleged confession of the murder of Mrs. Clyde Scranton, the night of January 29. Hill at the time of the alleged confession implicated Esque Warner, who is now serving a sentence at the Ohio State reformatory at Mansfield for attempting to attack Mrs. Margaret Christian a few nights after the Scranton murder.

The local officers will endeavor to corroborate the statement of Hill to the effect that he was in a hospital in Portsmouth January 30.

When Hill was arrested he had on his person a hospital certificate from a Portsmouth institution, stating that he had been admitted to the hospital January 30 and was discharged February 2. This hospital certificate showed that Hill was admitted as an employee of the N. & W. railroad, but the amount paid for care was only for two days. The officers are seeking to ascertain if the dates on the slip are correct and whether Hill was in Portsmouth the time of the murder.

In the *Marion Daily Star* on Thursday, March 13, 1919, Isaac Hill is still in the headlines. "HILL'S TALE OF SLAYING MRS. SCRANTON FALSE." The next smaller headline says, "Why Negro Spins Yarn Is Still a Mystery," followed by "BUT OFFICERS ATTRIBUTE IT TO HIS LOW MENTALITY" and by "Sheriff and Prosecutor Definitely Fix Hill's Presence in Portsmouth January 29."

The confession of Isaac Hill of the murder of Mrs. Clyde Scranton the night of January 29 was a pure lie," said Sheriff James F. Ullom today following his visit with Prosecuting Attorney Hector S. Young to Portsmouth yesterday.

The officers found that Hill was in Portsmouth January 29 and up to and including February 2. Previous to January 29 Hill had been in the employment of the Norfolk & Western railroad, the sheriff says.

The officers went to Portsmouth Tuesday night, taking Hill with them in an effort to find out when Hill was in a hospital at Portsmouth. When Hill was taken into custody one week ago Monday he had on his person a hospital certificate from a hospital at Portsmouth stating that he had been admitted to the institution January 30 and discharged February 2.

At the time of his arrest officers were at a loss to explain how Hill could have committed the murder in Marion the night of January 29 and then got to Portsmouth and be admitted to a hospital January 30.

A doctor of the N. & W. Railroad told the local officers that Hill had been treated by him for an injured hand January 27,

28 and 29 and that after January 29 he had heard no more from
him. The records of the hospital showed that Hill was admitted
to the institution January 31 and not January 30 as the hospital
discharge showed.

When the railroad doctor saw Hill he at once recognized him
as the man he had treated. The doctor scored Hill for not coming
back to him for further treatment and asked him what had become
of him. Hill then told him that he had been sent to a hospital and
after being discharged had come to Marion.

When Sheriff Ullom and Prosecutor Young asked Hill how he
was able to tell all the details of the Scranton murder Hill told
them that he had met a negro on the train, who had told him of
the crime and said that "Baby Face" or Esque Warner, was "in it."
From what Hill was told by the negro he was able to make up the
details of the crime, according to the officers.

When asked how he knew about the signet ring, Hill said that
the negro had told him that the ring together with other jewelry
had been taken from Mrs. Scranton by her assailant or assailants.
It was also developed by the officers that Hill had also lived on
Senate street here and from that knew the lay of the land in the
vicinity, where Mrs. Scranton was murdered.

Hill gave the officers no reason why he made the alleged
confession.

When the officers arrived at Portsmouth Hill was turned over
th the Portsmouth police who asked him to tell the story of the
murder. Hill again went through the details of the crime without
even a question from the officers.

Officers are at a loss to know how a man as ignorant as Hill
could have imagined all the details of the crime. Hill, officers say,
has no conception of time and is unable to count, yet he took the
officers over the scene of the crime and pointed out just where
the murder was committed and the route which Mrs. Scranton's
assailant or assailants took with the body after the attack. Officers
attribute his dream story to his low mentality.

Hill maintained the truth of his story until he was confronted
with the doctor who treated him at Portsmouth.

Hill is being held in the county jail pending an investigation
of his sanity.

The *Bucyrus News Forum* had two articles about Isaac Hill on the same day, Tuesday, March 11, 1919. The first had this headline: "Isaac Hill of Marion Held on Charge of Murder."
(United Press) Marion, March 7:

> Isaac Hill, colored, is being held on charges of being the slayer of Mrs. Clyde Scranton in this city on the night of January 29.
>
> Prosecutor Young stated today that Hill's confession implicated George Washington Warner, colored, who is serving a sentence in the Mansfield reformatory for an assault on Mrs. Margaret Christian.

The second article from the *Bucyrus News Forum* on Tuesday, March 11, 1919, had this headline: "Alleged Slayer of Marion Woman Worked Here."

> Isaac Hill, the negro held in Marion and alleged to have confessed to the murder of Mrs. Clyde Scranton in that city on the night of January 29, formerly worked in Bucyrus, and stayed here for some time, it was learned today. While in Bucyrus he boarded at a colored boarding in Oklahoma.
>
> Hill came here in the fall and began work at the Carroll Foundry and Machine Company plant, in the foundry department. He was however there only a few days, and then received his discharge papers on December 9th. After leaving the Carroll plant he worked for a while at the Steel plant, and went from there to Marion.

Our story about Isaac Hill continues with an article in the *Marion Daily Star* on Friday, March 14, 1919, and starts with this headline: "ISAAC HILL, NEGRO, CHAMPION DREAMER" then with "The Possibility of Electric Chair Doesn't Worry Him," followed by "BUT HE MUST HAVE TOTED RABBIT'S FOOT" and finally, "Anyhow, Charm of Some Kind Unmasks Falsity of His Murder Confession."

> "Well, sah boss, when Ah was picked up comin' to Marion, Ah thought Ah had to tell somethin' so Ah told about th' murder."

Isaac Hill, colored, told Prosecuting Attorney Hector S Young, today, after the prosecutor and Sheriff James F. Ullom had determined that Hill was not within 100 miles of Marion at the time Mrs. Clyde Scranton was murdered, January 29.

Prosecutor Young said today that Hill does not seem to realize what might have happened to him had not the officers found on his person a hospital certificate that he was in Portsmouth hospital January 30. When the officers told Hill that his confession might have sent him to the electric chair, Hill did not seem to realize what it meant.

Prosecutor Young said today that it was by mere chance that the falsity of Hill's story was found out at Portsmouth, where Prosecutor Young and Sheriff Ullom took Hill Wednesday.

The officers had established the fact that Hill had been treated in a hospital at Portsmouth previous to that date, and were just about to return to Marion, when Hill said to Prosecutor Young as they were passing a factory, that he had worked there.

The officers took him to the place and from officials there it was learned that Hill had been in their employ January 28, 29 and 30. Hill up to this time was still maintaining that he had committed the murder.

From officials at the place where Hill was working it was learned that he had been sent to a Y. M. C. A. First aid hospital for treatment of his hand. The officers at once went to the Y. M. C. A. hospital and there found the doctor who had treated Hill January 28, 29 and 30.

Hill told the prosecutor that he had learned all the details from a negro named "Roy" he met on a train en route from Portsmouth to West Virginia. He said that "Roy" was in Marion at the time all negroes had been ordered to leave the city.

Hill told the officers at Portsmouth that the week previous to his coming to Portsmouth he had walked from Kingston, West Virginia, to Portsmouth, a distance of 130 miles.

Hill is still being held in the county jail for safekeeping.

"Can you beat it?" Prosecutor Young smiled this morning when talking to newspapermen. Hill is classed as the champion dreamer.

The *Mansfield News* had an article about Isaac Hill on March 24, 1919, in a section of the paper called "NEWS FROM ROUND ABOUT BUCKEYE STATE."

Marion, March 24:

Isaac Hill, negro, is a puzzle. Innocent, he confessed to the atrocious murder of Mrs. Clyde Scranton, white, age 28, the evening of January 29, he stuck to his story implicating another negro now an inmate of the reformatory at Mansfield, until he was taken to Portsmouth, where he was faced by a hospital physician, who recognized him and said the negro had been under his care several days prior to the murder of Mrs. Scranton and for three days after. Hill then admitted he was lying.

A hospital discharge slip found in his pocket when arrested is what saved Hill. He had taken the officers over th scene of the murder and described in detail how he and his supposed accomplice had killed the woman. There were bits of corroborative evidence that would have sent him to the electric chair, Prosecuting Attorney Hector S. Young says. Had not the hospital slip been found, Hill would have been convicted of first degree murder on his own story, in many respects fully substantiated by the facts.

Mrs. Scranton's foul murder is just as much a mystery as it was the night they discovered her violated body. Two Cleveland detectives are working on the case. Authorities confess they are at sea.

Hill is still being held. Sheriff Ullom says he will not release him until ordered to do so by Prosecutor Young. Young says he will never order his release, because he is not safe to society. He cannot be sent to an asylum, because he is not insane. His disposition seems to be in the hands of the common pleas court.

CHAPTER 10

Steele and Dunlap

Before we return to the murder case, there are two items in the *Bucyrus Journal* and the *Mansfield News* that concern one of our principals in the murder case, and I include them here to provide a little background.

First from the *Bucyrus Journal* on Friday, February 28, 1919, we have this article with this headline: "DR. DUNLAP PROVES WHIRLWIND WOOER," then "Weds Mansfield Girl, 24 Hours After Meeting," and "BRIDE THEN RECONSIDERS." Then the article is preceded by this statement, "Learns That Husband is Spiritualist Which Shocks Her and She Sets Out to Get 'Character' from People Who Know Him._Matrimony Craft Kools Perilously But May Right Itself."

"Dr." Harry E. Dunlap of Bucyrus evidently proved to be a whirlwind wooer, that Mary Wise's wisdom was not keen enough to induce her to look up Mr. Dunlap in "Who's Who" before she took him as a life partner for better or worse.

All of which leads to rather an amazing story of the high speed courtship of "Dr." Dunlap which won the hand of Miss Wise, the latter a comely Mansfield girl of the brunette type, with a discriminating taste in dress.

"Dr." Dunlap is a spiritualist and clairvoyant, who has made Bucyrus his home for nearly two years, occupying rooms at the J. A. Nickelson residence at 419 North Walnut street. His new bride comes from a Mansfield family of good standing. Dr. Dunlap's second wife (this is his third marriage) died here last April.

According to seemingly authentic reports of what occurred last week, Dr. Dunlap was going someplace on a train and made the acquaintance of Miss Wise, who was a passenger on the same train, and whom he had never met before. Reports declare that Dunlap's wooing began promptly at first sight and with such a flying start not even the whole day elapsed before the twain were standing before the altar at the Methodist church in Mansfield, and were made one in wedlock by virtue of a ceremony by the pastor of that church, Rev. J. T. LeGear. The wedding occurred at 11 a. m. on Friday.

"Bride Gets to Thinking."

Dr. Dunlap, who gave his place of residence as Stratford, Canada, returned to Bucyrus Sunday, and went to his rooms at the Nickelson home. He announced to the family there that he had been married Friday at Mansfield.

Tuesday, his bride, her sister and a lady friend came to Bucyrus, with the avowed intention of finding out just who Dr. Dunlap is. It appears that the bride had not thought before learning anything of the past life of her new husband, nor of just who he was. The trio visited the Nickelson home; on learning that Dr. Dunlap had moved his quarters to the residence of Mrs. Rose Funk, 119 West Mary street they went to that address, but Dr. Dunlap happened to be out.

It is understood that those to whom the new Mrs. Dunlap talked gave Dr. Dunlap gave Dr. Dunlap a good character. It was learned then, that her chief cause for concern, and the motive prompting her to "look up" the doctor's record, was that she had discovered that he was a spiritualist. She does not believe in spiritualism and it is understood that she considered her new husband's method of earning a living rather precarious as to income, and preferred that he be engaged in something more stable.

While it was reported that Dunlap's bride had promptly announced her refusal to live with him, when she learned that he was a spiritualist, this belief conflicting with her religious convictions, it was stated that she is ready to accept her new husband if he will move to Mansfield and engage in another occupation.

So the whirlwind courtship may not result in an immediate smash on the matrimonial rocks, if the bride and groom can agree on a few little matters as to future course of action.

Then on another page of the *Bucyrus Journal* on the same date, Friday, February 28, 1919, we find this item with this headline: "DUNLAP NOW WANTS DIVORCE FROM MARY."

> "Dr." Harry Dunlap of this city, clairvoyant, has filed suit here for divorce from Mary Wise Dunlap, Mansfield girl he married on Feb. 14th after a one day acquaintance.
>
> He charges that she did not marry him in good faith, defrauded his rights, and is guilty of gross neglect.
>
> And the story continues . . .

From the *Mansfield News* on May 1, 1919, an article appeared with this bold headline: "UNHAPPY MARRIAGE." The smaller headline said, "Wife Says Husband Threatened to Kill Her."

> Mary Dunlap, in her petition for a divorce from Harry E. Dunlap says he assaulted her on their wedding day, choked her and threatened to kill her. They were married in this city Feb. 14. 1919.
>
> Mrs. Dunlap tells the common pleas court that before their marriage, her husband falsely represented to her that he was a doctor of medicine and a man of good repute. On the contrary, the wife says, his profession and practices for a livelihood were fraudulent, debasing and unscrupulous. She asks through her attorneys, Reed & Beach, that she be granted a divorce and be restored to her maiden name, Mary Wise. She also asks the court to grant her alimony.

Then on May 24, 1919, still from the *Mansfield News*, this report on the above divorce proceeding appeared with this headline: "Dunlap Replies."

> Harry E. Dunlap, gives his wife, Mary Dunlap, another chance, in his answer and cross petition filed in common pleas court. He says he has rooms furnished in Bucyrus for his wife and if she will come and live with him and perform her duties as a wife, he will perform all the duties of a husband.
>
> The husband denies all the material allegations in his wife's petition for divorce. He denies he has been guilty of gross neglect

of duty and charges that his wife persists in refusing to live with him. Dunlap says he purchased a apart of his wife's bridal outfit and has given her money at various times since their marriage.

Mrs. Dunlap in her petition charges her husband with gross neglect and asked to have her maiden name, Mary Wise, restored to her.

To continue the divorce case, in the *Mansfield News* on June 16, 1919, we find this headline and article: "Allowed Alimony."

Mary Wise Dunlap was allowed $50 alimony Saturday in common pleas court by Judge Galbraith, pending her suit for a divorce from her clairvoyant husband, Dr. Harry E. Dunlap of Bucyrus. Dr. Dunlap was in court and paid the alimony.

The Scranton murder case seems to have gone cold for a while. Our next item in the news that I have came on Tuesday, June 3, 1919, and had these headlines: "TWO NABBED IN WOMAN'S DEATH," which was followed by four smaller headlines. Next was "Arrests In Scranton Murder of January 29 Made Today," then "JAMES STEELE AND JOHN[1] DUNLAP ARE PRISONERS," followed by "Dunlap is a Chiropractor Residing at Bucyrus," ending with "He's Said To Be an Old Acquaintance of the Murdered WomanSteele is Railroad ManPrivate Detectives."

John Dunlap, chiropractor, of Bucyrus, and James Steele, Erie railroader, of this city, were arrested today by Sheriff James F. Ullom for the first-degree murder of Mrs. Clyde Scranton on the night of January 29. The affidavits were signed by George D. Tipton, of this city who has been working on the case since the murder. Dunlap was arrested at Bucyrus and Steele was arrested in this city.

The arrest came as a bombshell in local circles, as few knew that any detectives were working on the case. Tipton had as his coworker in the case Edward Dorward. Both men have followed many clews and finally this morning they went to Justice Charles W. Haberman's court and swore out affidavits against both men.

---

1.   This John Dunlap is Harry E. Dunlap

Sheriff Ullom and Constable D. S. Belt left early this morning to get Dunlap. They returned to Marion late this afternoon with the prisoner.

Steele was arrested last winter after the murder and was given the "third degree" by Prosecuting Attorney Hector S. Young in an effort to secure a confession, but at that time Steele protested his innocense and was later released. He was arrested at that time on a technical charge of carrying concealed weapons. This charge was ignored by the January grand jury.

According to the detectives, Dunlap was on the car that Mrs. Scranton returned to Marion on the night of the murder. The private detective also says that Dunlap got on the same local car that Mrs. Scranton took to west Center and Davids street and got off when Mrs. Scranton did.

The detectives say that Dunlap was an old acquaintance of Mrs. Scranton.

The men under arrest stoutly maintain they are innocent.

The murder of Mrs. Scranton has been one of the most baffling in local police circles. Mrs. Scranton was found on a coal pile to the west of the Erie roundhouse about 9:30 at night. At the time she was found the body was still warm.

At the autopsy the coroner found that her death had been caused by a blow over the head and also by being strangled.

The last time Mrs. Scranton was seen the night of the murder was when she alighted from a city street car at Davids and west Center streets. She was attacked a few yards from her home on Cass avenue. The body was then taken across fields and over fences the Erie coal pile.

The only clew that officials found at the time of the murder was the statement of Mrs. L. B. Lessig, a neighbor who was keeping the Scranton children. She heard a scream about the time the murder was supposed to have taken place, but made no investigation.

At the place where Mrs. Scranton was attacked her hat, muff and handkerchief were found. Mrs. Scranton had been at Bucyrus on business for the National Protective Legion and returned to Marion about 8 o'clock in the evening.

On her arrival here she called her home and asked Mrs. Lessig to turn on the porch light as she was afraid. Mr. Scranton was attending an Erie meeting.

When Mrs. Scranton did not return home Mrs. Lessig became alarmed and a search was instituted. When the handkerchief, hat and muff were found, people at once became suspicious of foul play.

Mrs. Scranton was found by Steele and Elmer Patten.

Following the murder people became inflamed against the colored population and an exodus of all colored people followed.

Our next item was in *The Marion Daily Star* on Wednesday, June 4, 1919, and had these headlines: "MORE ARRESTS COMING IN MURDER OF WOMAN," followed by "Number Under Surveillance in Scranton Crime Mystery," then "DECLARE DETECTIVES WORKING ON THE CASE," and "Details Leading Up to the Arrest of James Steele and John Dunlap."

More arrests are expected to follow in the Scranton murder case, according to Detectives Edward Dorward and George D. Tipton. A number of persons, who are thought to know considerable about it, are under surveillance.

Following the arrests of James Steele, an Erie worker, at the Erie roundhouse, late yesterday afternoon, and John Dunlap, chiropractor, of Bucyrus, earlier in the day, a number of people called the detectives and gave them valuable information regarding the murder.

The detectives state that a number of people who know facts have now voluntarily given information that will have an important bearing on the case.

Dunlap was arrested yesterday morning near Nevada by Constable D. S. Belt, of Justice Charles W. Haberman's court. Constable Belt and Sheriff James F. Ullom, together with Detective Tipton, went to Bucyrus early yesterday morning.

Dunlap had gone fishing and the officers started in search of him. He was finally located along a stream near Nevada. When arrested Dunlap protested his innocense.

When Dunlap was taken to his home before being brought to Marion his family had a complete alibi for his whereabouts on the night of January 29, the night of the murder. Later, on his way to Marion, Dunlap, the arresting officers say, admitted being here, saying he came to this city on a business trip.

When Steele was arrested his only comment was: "Don't this beat hell!" Steele was taken into custody as he reported to work yesterday at 3 o'clock.

The first clew that the detectives secured when they started to work on the case last April was a chance remark that was dropped by a man, at whose home Dunlap is alleged to have stayed the night of the murder. The name of this man is being kept secret at the request of the officers.

From this remark the officers learned that Dunlap had been in Marion the night of the murder and had taken the same car, west as did Mrs. Scranton, the detectives claim.

The detectives further state that Dunlap came to Marion on the same interurban car as Mrs. Scranton and accompanied her to Schmidt's drug store, where she called her home and asked to have the porch light turned on.

In the store Dunlap had a $20 bill changed and gave eight dollars to the mysterious man, whose chance remark gave the officers the first tip. Dunlap and Mrs. Scranton was in the store about 8:03 o'clock, authorities say.

Mrs. Scranton left the store alone, according to the detectives. A few moments later, in company with the "mysterious man," walked east on Center street to the Columbia theater, where Dunlap said he thought he would take the car west. (The Columbia Theater was located at 127 E. Center Street.)

Detectives say Mrs. Scranton was on this car. The car started west about 8:05 o'clock. A number of people, detectives say, will testify they saw Mrs. Scranton and Dunlap on this car.

The car reached Davids and Center streets about 8:15 o'clock. Mrs. Scranton and Dunlap alighted here, according to the detectives story. Dunlap, they say, tarried here.

At 8:17 o'clock, according to the detectives, Mrs. Scranton reached the Erie railroad crossing, where she was held up on account of a switch engine. The detectives say that both the fireman and engineer talked with Mrs. Scranton, while waiting for track to be cleared. Dunlap is alleged to have caught up with Mrs. Scranton. He was then seen by the engineer and fireman, according to the detectives.

A short time later two or three people, who are known to the detectives, that he men were fighting and a woman was in between them. They saw her fall to the ground, but made no investigation.

A little while later two people, detectives state, saw two men carrying something across Kenton avenue. The murder is thought to have been committed between 8:20 and 8:50 o'clock, according to detectives.

The night of the murder there was a meeting of engine inspectors at the Erie master mechanic's office. According to the detectives Steele went to the meeting with five other men, but did not sit with them. He stood in the door.

Steele was one of the speakers at the meeting. He was called on about 8:50 o'clock, according to the detectives. Men who were at the meeting say that when he took the floor he was so excited he could hardly talk, according to detectives.

When the telephone rang, Steele is said to have stopped in the middle of his speech, took his hat and coat and hurriedly left. He talked only about two minutes, according to the detectives. The telephone call was for Mr. Scranton, who was told that his wife was missing.

Mrs. Scranton's body was found about half an hour later by Steele with another man named Elmer Patten. According to the detectives Steele told the police that when he found Mrs. Scranton's body her clothes were mussed, but Patten told the detectives that this was not the case. Patten states, according to the detectives, that her clothes were neatly smoothed out and her coat buttoned.

When the police patrol arrived it could only get within 100 feet of the body. Steele helped to carry the body to the patrol wagon, according to the detectives. After the body had been placed in the wagon Steele is alleged to have said: "I lost my coat." He started in search of it and found it about eight feet from the place where the body was first found, according to the detectives.

Detectives say that they found Steele's pipe near the body. They also state that a few days after the murder Steele took a negro over the route the body was taken the night of the murder.

This information was obtained from Isaac Hill, who confessed to the officers that he committed the murder, but whose confession was later discredited.

Detectives say they expect to arrest the negro in a few days.

Officers stated that when Dunlap was arrested yesterday he showed no surprise. Coming to Marion they say he made a number of statements regarding the murder which officers say were true.

Dunlap and Steele are being kept apart at the county jail.

Dorward is lieutenant of the watch at the Marion Steam Shovel company's plant and Tipton is employed at night at the Erie freight house.

Steele refused to talk about the case when placed under arrest yesterday.

It was interesting to me that on Friday, February 6, 1919, the *Bucyrus News Forum* ran a story identical to the last word of the article in the *Marion Daily Star* immediately above. This Marion murder story was getting a lot of coverage in other towns. The only difference was this headline in Bucyrus: "MORE ARRESTS ARE EXPECTED AT MARION IN SCRANTON CASE."

CHAPTER 11

The Husband of Rose Belle

Then the next day, the *Marion Daily Star*, Thursday, June 5, 1919, had this to report on the continuing narrative of this murder mystery. The headline of this article I'm sure got Marion's attention. The first headline was "SCRANTON HELD AS WIFE SLAYER," followed by "Woman Detective Charges Him with Crime January 29," then "DEAD WOMAN'S HUSBAND TAKEN LATE LAST NIGHT," then a smaller, "Declares He is Innocent and Is Not Excited." And the final headline states, "Events Move Rapidly in Scranton Murder MysteryDunlap, Also Held, a clairvoyant Visits Steele in Jail."

Another sensational development in the Scranton murder case was sprung last night at midnight, when Clyde

Scranton, husband of the murdered woman was placed under arrest charged with her murder, the night of January 29.

The arrest was made by Sheriff James F. Ullom and Patrolman Walter Perratt. Scranton was at the home of Don Hoagland, a relative, corner of Bennett and LaTourette streets.

The affidavit for the arrest was signed by Mrs. M. E. Fritzinger, a detective who has been working on the case fo some months. She was formerly employed by Prosecuting Attorney Hector S. Young.

The affidavit was secured in Justice Charles W. Haberman's court last night about 10 o'clock.

When arrested Scranton had nothing to say, but appeared very nervous, but unexcited.

Mrs. Fritzinger claims to have knowledge of many circumstances that throw much light on the crime.

It is claimed that two Columbus negroes, Roy Kalow, and another named Williams, passed the Scranton home on the night of the murder and saw a woman about the size of Mrs. Scranton enter the house.

Mrs. Fritzinger says that while in Columbus sometime ago in search of Kalow, she went to Joe White's saloon. There she inquired for Kalow and in conversation with Williams he told her that he and Kalow were in Marion the night of the murder, and had seen the woman answering Mrs. Scranton's description.

Mrs. Fritzinger says the two negroes saw a man carrying what they thought to be a small child in his arms through the weeds in the rear of the Scranton home.

Mrs. Fritzinger claims that when Mrs. Scranton's hat and muff were found a few yards from the Scranton home the hat was on top of the muff as though it had been placed there, indicating there was no struggle. The theory of the police at the time of the murder was that Mrs. Scranton had been attacked near where the hat and muff were found. It is also pointed out by Mrs. Fritzinger that the autopsy revealed bits of pickles, ham and bread in Mrs. Scranton's windpipe and throat, as though she had been choked.

Mrs. L. B. Lessig, a neighbor, who was at the Scranton home the night of the murder and who kept the Scranton children, states that they had for supper that evening, ham, pickles and bread, according to the woman detective.. Mrs. Scranton did not arrive home from Bucyrus that fatal night until 8 o'clock.

Mrs. Lessig was not at the Scranton home at the time, according to the detective, having gone home to get her husband's supper.

Another link in the chain of evidence, according to Mrs. Fritzinger, is that a hair switch, which Mrs. Scranton is said to have worn when she left home the morning of the murder, was found behind a picture in the Scranton home.

It is claimed that Scranton did not go to the meeting at the master mechanic's office at the Erie until late the night of the murder.

Scranton when he was called to the telephone and was told his wife was missing went home. He did not go out in search of his wife, the detective states, but remained in the house together with N. D. Noggle, who accompanied him home from the meeting.

Scranton claims the reason he remained home was that Noggle told him it would be better to stay in the house near the telephone so that as soon as Mrs. Scranton was found they could be easily reached. Scranton claims to have wanted to go out and search for his wife, but that Noggle would not let him.

It is claimed by Mrs. Fritzinger that while the search for Mrs. Scranton was going on Steele, who was arrested Tuesday afternoon charged with the crime, came to the Scranton home and called Scranton out on the front porch.

Mrs. Fritzinger states that Scranton and Steele had a conversation and later Steele found the body.

Scranton told reporters last night that about the middle of February he was going to the Hoagland home and on Bennett street Steele caught up with him. Scranton stopped and talked with Steele. Scranton says that while talking to Steele he looked down at Steele's pocket and saw a gun sticking out.

Scranton asked if he had any fear of Steele stated he did not, but a little later he said he felt more at ease when Steele was locked up.

Scranton denied that he had ever had any domestic troubles and said: A better woman never walked in shoe leather. We lived together about eight years and in all that time never had any trouble."

Scranton said that on two occasions Steele had accompanied Mrs. Scranton home from lodge meeting, but that his wife had asked him, Scranton, if he objected and Scranton said he did not. Scranton claims he always met his wife except on two occasions.

Edward Dorward, who has been working on the case and who with George Tipton, caused the arrest of Steele and "Dr." Harry Dunlap, of Bucyrus, last Tuesday, stated last night that Charles Corbin, an Erie employee, saw two men carrying something resembling a body across Kenton avenue about 8:20 o'clock, he says.

A number of other people who may throw light on the case have volunteered information in the past few days to the detectives working on the mystery. Several people who claim to know of incidents leading up to the murder have given data to the detectives, according to Dorward and Tipton.

A thorough investigation is being made of all the information by these two detectives, who believe that they are drawing the net around the party or parties guilty of the crime.

If sufficient evidenced is adduced at the preliminary hearings of the men in Justice Haberman's court to hold them to the grand jury, Judge Mouser announced late yesterday that the grand jury will be called in special session.

Scranton denies knowing anything about the crime and declares he is innocent.

Last night the wife of James Steele was permitted to see him at the county jail.

According to the Bucyrus newspapers Dunlap's right name is Harry E. Dunlap. It is stated at Bucyrus that he is a clairvoyant medium and that he is not a doctor.

Speaking of Dunlap's arrest Wednesday's *Bucyrus Telegraph* said:

Dunlap has roomed with Mrs. Rose Funk, No. 119 west Mary street, Bucyrus, since last September. Previous to that he roomed at the J. P. Nickelson residence, No. 419 north Walnut, where his first wife died.

Mrs. Funk, interviewed today by the Telegraph, said Dunlap was very irregular in his comings and goings, rarely being in his room more than a few nights a week. He has not been there since Sunday. She expected him back tonight. He often made trips to the country, frequently to the Dan Steiger home near Nevada.

Dunlap was married a few months after the death of his first wife to Mary Wise, of Mansfield, whom he had met only the day before. He sought a divorce in February, just a few weeks after their marriage, as she declined to live with him.

Mrs. L. B. Lessig, of Cass avenue, said this morning that while the search for Mrs. Scranton's body was on Scranton had Steele called on the telephone and asked him to come over to the house.

Mrs. Lessig states that Scranton held a conversation with Steele and a little while later Steele returned to the Scranton home and said he had found a body on a coal pile near the Erie roundhouse.

It was stated by Mrs. Lessig this morning that when Steele returned to the house Scranton asked him if he had found the body. Steele said "yes," and continued saying that he had covered it with his overcoat.

Mrs. Steele when seen this morning stated that a grave injustice had been done to her husband by his arrest. Mrs. Steele states that she is positive her husband knows nothing of the murder. Steele protests his innocence and tells the officers he knows nothing of the crime or of anything that would lead to the apprehension of the slayer or slayers.

Mrs. Steele is heartbroken. She told interviewers that she felt her husband was being made the "goat" for other people who knew about the murder. Mrs. Steele says that her husband and Scranton were the best of friends up to the time Steele was arrested.

Mrs. Lessig gave this morning a detailed history of the murder. She stated that Mrs. Scranton had asked her the morning of the murder to stay with the children during the day. Mrs. Lessig stated Mrs. Scranton gave her $1.50 for keeping the children.

Mrs. Lessig, according to her story, went to the Scranton house early in the morning. When she arrived Mrs. Scranton was upstairs completing her toilet.

Mrs. Scranton asked Mrs. Lessig to brush her hat and coat and after some instructions about the children and an errand, Mrs. Scranton left.

A little while later Mrs. Scranton called her on the telephone and asked her not to forget the errand. Mrs. Scranton told Mrs. Lessig that if she were not able to get back from Bucyrus she would telephone.

Mrs. Lessig states she kept the children all day. About 3 o'clock in the afternoon Scranton returned home from work. He remained about the house the remainder of the afternoon.

When Mrs. Scranton did not return from Bucyrus on the six o'clock car. Mr. Scranton asked Mrs. Lessig if she would stay with the children that evening, as he had to go to a meeting of the Erie inspectors. Mrs. Lessig went to the Scranton home about 7:30 o'clock, just as Mr. Scranton was leaving.

Shortly before 8 o'clock, while Mrs. Lessig was putting the children to bed, Mrs. Scranton called and said something about her sister, which Mrs. Lessig can not remember. In the conversation she asked Mrs. Lessig to turn on the porch light, as she said she was afraid to come home. Mrs. Lessig had told Mrs. Scranton that her husband was at a meeting and could not meet her.

A short time later Mrs. Lessig heard someone say "Oh!" in a manner of Mrs. Scranton. A boy, who had brought the washing, was at the Scranton home at the time and remarked about it, but no investigation was made of it. Mrs. Lessig states that the reason she did not make an investigation was because she thought that possibly it was some one else because Mrs. Scranton did not come.

Mrs. Lessig states that just before the hat and muff were found she heard people walking by the house and talking. A little while later they brought in the hat and muff and when she examined them and knew they were the ones Mrs. Scranton had worn away that morning she said: "My God! Something awful has happened to Mrs. Scranton. Call the police!"

Mrs. Lessig then had Mr. Scranton called and he came home with N. D. Noggle. Mrs. Lessig states that Mr. Scranton was very much excited and sat in a chair crying. She states he did not go out to hunt his wife. Once, Mrs. Lessig states, he wanted to go, but Noggle told him he had better stay home, as there were enough out hunting for his wife's body.

Mrs. Lessig then told how Scranton had Steele called, and the conversation and the finding of the body later.

Mrs. Lessig stoutly denies that Mrs. Scranton's switch, which Mrs. Scranton wore was found in the house. She says it was brought home from the undertakers. An officer states that when Mrs. Scranton was taken to the hospital, before being removed to the undertaking establishment of Hess & Markert, she did not have the hair switch on.

Mrs. Lessig says that she did not get supper for Mrs. Scranton, but cleared up the table when she returned to the Scranton home after the evening meal.

Mrs. Lessig states that Scranton was not in the house after he left until he came home when he had been called, following the finding of her hat and muff. She states that as far as she knew Mr. And Mrs. Scranton had always got along excellently and so far as she knew had never had any trouble.

Dunlap, of Bucyrus, it is said is a former Marion man, having lived here about eight years ago. He was at that time employed as a carpenter. He has lived in Bucyrus about two years.

The above article also appeared word for word in the *Bucyrus News Forum* on Tuesday, June 10, 1919, the only difference being the headline. In the *News Forum*, the headline read, "Woman Detective Causes the Arrest of Clyde Scranton in Marion Murder Case Today."

CHAPTER 12

The Reward

The Friday, June 6, 1919, *Marion Daily Star* had this to report with this headline: "LARGER REWARD MAY BE MADE TO SOLVE MYSTERY," then "With View To Attracting Best Detective Talent," followed by "PRESENT REWARD NOW OFFERED IS $1,000," and "Dunlap, One of Alleged Trio of Slayers, Will Be Given Preliminary Hearing Tomorrow."

It was said yesterday afternoon that the county commissioners may offer a large reward for the arrest and conviction of the slayer or slayers of Mrs. Clyde Scranton, whose body was found near the Erie roundhouse, January 29.

The commissioners, a short time after the discovery of the crime, offered a reward of $1,000. This, it was thought at the time, would attract reliable detectives over the country, but it has failed to do so and hence there is much talk among many interested in the case of increasing the reward to such a figure that the best sleuths in the country will be attracted by it. A former prosecuting attorney yesterday expressed himself to the effect that such a reward should be offered. It has been suggested that a reward of $5,000 would be sufficient to get the country's best detective talent.

The matter will be taken up with the commissioners, it was said by officials today. Those who are urging a larger reward point out that it would be cheaper to offer a larger reward than to pay detectives who work on the case.

Officials claim that $1,000 would soon be spent for detectives if they were employed by some agency. One experienced official stated that by offering a reward of $5,000 big detectives over the country would come to the city and work on the mystery.

Thursday's June 5, 1919, *Bucyrus Telegraph* has the following about Harry E. Dunlap of Bucyrus who is held here on a charge of slaying Mrs. Scranton:

More has been learned about the clairvoyant, Dunlap, whose headquarters has been in Bucyrus for two years, and whose age is about forty. It develops that he was working at the carpenter trade at Marion eight years ago, and later developed his "mediumistic" tendency. It has always been understood here that he came from Canton. He married a Bucyrus woman who died in a little over a year. A short time elapsed between her death and the whirlwind twenty-four-hour courtship in which he won and married Mary Wise, of Mansfield.

An examination of the records shows that Dunlap was not awarded a divorce, but that on April 11, he had the case dismissed at his own costs. The Scranton woman's murder occurred January 29. On February 14, Dunlap married the Wise girl. They separated once and on February 24 he sued for divorce, alleging fraud, on the ground that the Wise girl had not married him in good faith. She is now suing him for alimony and he is reported to have been writing to her quite frequently.

If Dunlap actually had a hand in the killing of Rose Scranton, he went on to his second marriage bloody-handed, only fifteen days after the murder.

A Telegraph reporter had a glimpse of Dunlap's room at the Funk residence on west Mary street Wednesday. On the north wall is a handsomely-framed photograph of Dunlap and his dead wife. There are two trunks in the room, one a comparatively new one. A pair of new tan oxfords under the bed, a soft hat thrown on the trunk and some outer clothing carelessly pitched over another; along with a quart wine bottle, empty, four or five boxes of matches, some clean shirts on an island, a camera and box of films and a dresser with quite an array of toilet articles on its top, presenting nothing out of the ordinary. Mrs. Funk says the officers did not inspect Dunlap's room. She says she has five boarders and that Dunlap always behaved himself there or she would not have had him.

Dunlap's photo shows him to be a pleasing appearing person. He is of medium height, rather heavy-set, black hair, smooth face and dresses well always.

Mrs. L. B. Lessig, of Cass avenue, who kept the children January 29, today denied that she had said that when James Steele, now under arrest, returned to the Scranton house, Scranton asked him if he had found he body. Steele was quoted by her as saying "yes" in reply. Steele added that he had covered the body with his coat. Mrs. Lessig denies she ever said this.

Mrs. Lessig further says that Scranton came home in the afternoon about 3 o'clock, washed and then went away. He was gone about two hours. Upon his return Mrs. Lessig then went to her own home, returning to the Scranton home about 7:30 o'clock. She says that Scranton did not ask her to keep the children while he attended the meeting of railroad inspectors, but that she volunteered to keep them for him and told him to go and attend the meeting. Lessig also states that while she did prepare the evening meal at the Scranton home she cleared up the table and knows that they only had a light lunch of pineapples, milk, butter and bread.

"Dr." Harry Dunlap, of Bucyrus, will be the first of the three men who have been arrested charged with the murder of Mrs. Scranton, to be arraigned. Dunlap will be arraigned in Justice Charles W. Haberman's court tomorrow afternoon.

Thirty-two witnesses have been subpoenaed to appear at the hearing tomorrow afternoon.

Officers said this morning that they have a number of people under surveillance who they believe know something about the murder. Officers say the people are being shadowed so that in the event they attempt to leave the city they can be placed under arrest.

Last evening Scranton at the county jail again went over with officers the details of his actions the night of the murder and persisted he knows nothing more than he has already told. Scranton has retained James H. Eymon to defend him. Steele also stoutly disclaims any connection with the crime and says he knows nothing that will throw any light on it. He is represented by Attorney William P. Moloney.

The following persons have been subpoenaed to appear at the preliminary hearing of Dunlap: Elmer Patten, Nochious D. Noggle, H. S. Scoville, Mrs. Duffey of Cass avenue, Mrs. L. B. Lessig, Charles Corbin, Mrs. Otis Leeper, Mrs. Frank Read, Mrs. Joseph Johnson, Mrs. Wilhelm of Creston avenue, John Wren, J. W. Thompson, Perry Baker, Goldie Fosnaugh, Bliss Hoagland, Don Hoagland, Mrs. George Landon, Katie Baker, Lewis Gear, Frank Schultz, Mrs. Frank Shultz, Henry Baker, Mr. Willie, William Sagers, Inter Esbam, Deven Tromte, William Latham, Mrs. Snyder of Cass avenue, Ivan Shaw, Mrs. Ivan Shaw, George Coffee and William Baker.

From the *Steubenville Herald-Star* also on June 5, 1919, we find this headline and article: "HUSBAND ACCUSED."

Marion, Ohio, June 5:

Clyde Scranton, husband of Rosa Scranton, who was murdered here January 29, was arrested last night charged with the murder of his wife. Scranton an Erie car inspector, protests his innocence. Scranton's arrest was brought about through a woman detective who says the evidence collected by her tends to show Mrs. Scranton was murdered in her home and her body was found on a dump near the railroad yards.

Dr. John Dunlap, of Bucyrus, and James Steele of Marion, Erie railroaders are already in jail here charged with Mrs Scranton's murder, affidavits against them having been filed by detectives George Tipton and Edward Dorward.

The *Mansfield News* of June 6, 1919, had this coverage with this headline: "CHARGE MARION MAN WITH WIFE'S MURDER" with this smaller headline, "Clyde Scranton Third to be Arrested This Week in Connection With Crime."

Clyde Scranton, husband of Rosa Scranton, who was murdered at Marion on the night of January 29, was arrested at Marion yesterday charged with the murder of his wife. Scranton, who is an Erie railroad inspector, protested his innocence.

Scranton's arrest was accomplished through a woman detective, Mrs. M. E. Fritzinger, who claims that evidence will be produced to show that Mrs. Scranton was killed in her own home. She also indicates that an effort will be made to prove that the dead woman was strangled to death by having pickles, bread and ham forced down her throat and into her windpipe. She points to the coroner's autopsy as showing that particles of these foods were found in the dead woman's windpipe, and indicates that it can be proven that these articles were served at supper at the Scranton home the night of the murder. Witnesses have been found it is declared, who saw Mrs. Scranton enter her home after 8 p. m., and who afterward saw a man carrying something, thought to be a child across lots from that vicinity not long afterwards.

Scranton's arrest is believed to be on the strength of a belief that he was in a plan to murder his wife, even if he did not have a hand in the actual killing.

Those who have been attracted by the sensational developments in the murder case, bringing the arrest of three men in quick succession, are puzzled at the new developments. Scranton has been understood to have been attending a railroad foreman's meeting at the hour the killing must have occurred. If this is true, he was an alibi as far as the actual killing of the woman is concerned. But the belief that he was involved in a deliberate plan to make away with his wife seems to be at the bottom of his arrest.

From the *Marion Daily Star* on Saturday, June 7, 1919, we find these headlines and article. "PRELIMINARY HEARINGS IN MURDER CASE MONDAY," then "Habeas Corpus Proceedings Are Threatened, It's Claimed," followed by "WOMAN DETECTIVE SAYS SHE CAN'T BE READY BY THEN." Finally, we have "Mother, Important Witness, Ill. New Bits of Evidence—About That Larger Reward."

Preliminary hearings of Clyde Scranton, James Steele and "Dr." Harry Dunlap will likely be held Monday morning in Justice Charles W. Haberman's court, it was announced today by Justice Haberman.

All three men are now in the county jail charged with the murder of Mrs. Clyde Scranton the night of January 29.

Justice Haberman said the hearing was being held Monday to offset threatening habeas corpus proceedings. About forty witnesses have been subpoenaed to appear in the Steele and Dunlap hearing.

Mrs. M. E. Fritzinger, who signed the affidavit for the arrest of Scranton, said this morning she would be unable to have her witnesses in the city Monday. Mrs. Fritzinger says her mother is an important witness in the case.

Detectives Edward Dorward and George Tipton, who caused the arrest of Steele and Dunlap, say they are ready to produce their witnesses Monday.

Detectives who have been working on the case of Steele and Dunlap announced this morning that two important pieces of evidence have been unearthed.

Detectives refused to divulge the exact nature of the evidence, but said both went to the actions of James Steele and "Dr." Harry Dunlap since the murder. One came in the form of a letter, it is said, from a city not far from Marion telling of Dunbar's mysterious actions.

The other piece of evidence the detectives refused to talk about saying that it would have a material bearing on the case.

The hearing of Scranton, which was to have been held this afternoon, was postponed on account of the failure to get a number of the witnesses, who live outside of Marion county, here in time.

The Kenton News Republican in telling of the murder and developments in the case says: "It is likely that popular opinion will compel Marion county commissioners to increase the reward of $1,000 which was offered for the slayer of Mrs. Scranton. The public of Marion county is demanding the apprehension of the slayer or slayers of the woman, and the commissioners will likely have to make the reward offered larger, although they do not appear willing to do so. A larger reward, it is held, will attract the best detective talent to work on the case.

Then from the *Mansfield News* also on June 7, 1919, this headline and story appeared: "ASK LARGER REWARD" followed by "Marion Officials Would Make Effort to Solve Mystery."

Marion officials are making an effort to have the Marion county commissioners offer a larger reward for the conviction of those responsible for the murder of Mrs. Rosa Scranton at Marion January 29. They seek to have the reward increased from $1,000 to $5,000. They believe that this would attract prominent detectives to the case and help solve the mystery.

"Dr." Harry Dunlap, of Bucyrus, will be the first of the three men arrested this week in connection with the case to be arraigned. Thirty-two witnesses have been summoned for the trial to be held this afternoon before Justice C. W. Haberman. Clyde Scranton and James Steele will have their hearings next week.

Officers at Marion stated yesterday that they have a number of people under surveillance who they believe know something about the murder. These people are being shadowed, and if they attempt to leave Marion they will be placed under arrest.

From the *Marion Daily Star* on Monday, June 9, 1919, these headlines and story appeared.

First headline was "DUNLAP PRELIMINARY HEARING IS ON TODAY," then "Some Conflict in Testimony as to Dunlap's Visit Here," followed by "SCRANTON'S HEARING IS CONTINUED TO WEDNESDAY," and "Dunlap Suffers Collapse Saturday—Trunkful of Letters Is Found—The Testimony."

Dr. Harry Dunlap, of Bucyrus, is being given a preliminary examination in Justice Haberman's court this afternoon on a charge of the first-degree murder of Mrs. Clyde Scranton, the night of January 29.

The hearing is being held in the common pleas courtroom in order to accommodate the crowd, which is attending the hearing.

The first witness called was Mrs. Frank Schultz, of north Greenwood street, at whose home it is claimed Dunlap was the night of the murder. Mrs. Schultz described Dunlap coming to the home about 6 o'clock in the evening. She said he seemed very nervous. She testified Dunlap said he came to Marion from Bucyrus on the car, but didn't say what time he arrived here. He told the Schultz family he was sick and had come for some medicine, Mrs. Schultz testified.

Mrs. Schultz testified Dunlap mentioned, in a conversation at the Schultz home he met an insurance woman on the car. Mrs. Shultz he did not say who it was, but said she was "a nice looking little woman." She did not think he meant Mrs. Scranton. She said he remained at the Schultz home about a half hour.

The witnesses testified Dunlap then left with Mr. Shultz and went down town to a drug store. Mrs. Schultz said her son, John, was at home when Dunlap was there. When asked where John was now Mrs. Schultz said she did not know.

In the examination, which was conducted by Attorney James H. Eymon, Mrs. Schultz placed the date when Dunlap was at her home on January 27.

Attorney Eymon in his examination attempted to bring out that Mrs. Schultz last week told him and George Tipton it was January 29 when Dunlap was there instead of January 27. Mr. Eymon asked Mrs. Schultz why it was when he was at the Schultz home last week Mrs. Schultz argued with her husband it was January 29 when her husband said it was January 27.

Sheriff James F. Ullom was the next witness called. He testified Dunlap told him in the presence of other persons that he came to Marion January 29 on the eight o'clock interurban car from Bucyrus and left on the nine o'clock car.

Sheriff Ullom testified Dunlap said he came here to see a doctor whose name he did not remember. He testified Dunlap accounted for every minute of his time while in Marion and when it was added up it totaled two hours.

Sheriff Ullom testified Dunlap said he got off the car and went to a grocer and he inquired where the doctor lived. He said Dunlap told him he gave a boy twenty-five or fifty cents to take him to the Schultz home. Dunlap told the sheriff the exact time he was at each place and his every movement while in Marion.

Dunlap told the sheriff, according to Sheriff Ullom's testimony, he went to the Schmidt drug store and got a bill changed and gave some of the money to Mr. Schultz for some medicine.

Sheriff Ullom testified Dunlap said he was in Marion January 29.

Dunlap is represented by Attorney L. C. Feighner, of Bucyrus.

Following the examination of Dunlap James Steele will be given a preliminary hearing. Steele is being held to answer the same charge as Dunlap.

Dunlap suffered a nervous collapse late Saturday afternoon following a grilling by detectives working on the case. Dunlap's condition became so bad Sheriff James F. Ullom was forced to call a physician. Dunlap recovered somewhat yesterday, but a doctor again waited on him yesterday morning. For a time Saturday afternoon, Sheriff Ullom said it was feared that Dunlap would die.

The hearing of Clyde Scranton, husband of the murdered woman, which was to have been held this morning at 9 o'clock in Justice Charles W. Haberman's court, was continued until

Wednesday morning. The continuance was given at the request of Mrs. M. E. Fritzinger, a detective, who caused the arrest of Scranton.

Mrs. Fritzinger stated to the court that she was unable to get some of her important witnesses here this morning in time for the hearing.

James H. Eymon, counsel for Scranton, objected to a continuance.

A trunkful of correspondence was found in "Dr." Harry Dunlap's room at Bucyrus, Saturday afternoon, it is claimed by Detective Edward Dorward, who has been working on the solution of the Scranton murder mystery. Detective Dorward said this morning Dunlap had letters from girls and women all over the central part of the state.

In Dunlap's trunk was also found a large number of pictures of women and girls. Detective Dorward said that Dunlap must have occupied the larger part of his spare time writing letters from the amount of correspondence found in his room. The trunk in which the letters and pictures were found had been broken open before the detectives arrived, Dorward said this morning.

Justice Haberman's office was filled with spectators this morning to hear the preliminary examination of Scranton.

The very next day in the *Marion Daily Star*, June 10, 1919, we have this story with these headlines in large bold print: "DUNLAP AND STEELE ARE FULLY EXONERATED," followed by "Freed of Murder Charge Upon Motion of J. H. Eymon," then another in capital letters, "SAYS STATE'S WITNESSES TELL DIFFERENT STORIES," and "Scranton, Husband of Slain Woman, Released on Personal Bond of $5,000."

After Attorney James E. Eymon, who represented Edward Dorward and George Tipton, private detectives, who caused the arrest of James Steele, Marion, Erie mechanic, and Harry E. Dunlap, of Bucyrus, held on a charge of the first-degree murder of Mrs. Clyde Scranton, had exonerated both men from the charge in open court, Justice Charles W. Haberman, late yesterday afternoon, dismissed both men.

Justice Haberman found that there was no probable cause to bind the men over to the grand jury. Justice Haberman also fixed the bond of Clyde Scranton, husband of the murdered woman, held at the county jail since last Wednesday to answer to the same charge, at $5,000. Scranton furnished personal bond and was released last evening.

Scranton was arrested on an affidavit signed by Mrs. M. E. Fritzinger, a private detective. Scranton's hearing, which was to have been held yesterday, will be held Wednesday morning.

In his statement to the court asking that the charges be dismissed, Attorney Eymon said that if the people who had talked to him and the two detectives, who had caused the arrest of Steele and Dunlap, had told one-tenth the truth on the witness stand they had told privately, the court would have been forced to bind both men over to the grand jury.

"It is either one of two things," Attorney Eymon said, "they did not tell us the truth or they perjured themselves on the witness stand."

"These men who caused the arrest of the accused," Attorney Eymon continued, "went into this case because of the interest of the community in unraveling the mystery."

"These two men can not be censured by the two defendants, because I myself have talked to many of the witnesses who have been called in the case and have heard their story and if they had told the same story on the witness stand they told us, these two men would have been bound over."

"Witnesses have come into court in this case and either fall down on the story they were supposed to have told, or make their stories differ so much, they either prevaricated to us or did not tell the truth under oath."

"There is one thing that I wish it were possible to impress on their minds, and that is that when a man is charged with first-degree murder there should be something against him. The men who caused the arrest of Steele and Dunlap were acting in good faith and were justified in filing affidavits and it is no more than right to say there is no evidence to bind the defendants over and that they are exonerated."

"I can't understand how people could tell me and these other men who have been working on the case stories like they did and then when they get on the stand they go back into their shell and won't tell anything."

Evidence introduced at the hearing yesterday afternoon in no way implicated either Dunlap or Steele. Fred Flocken, druggist, testified that Frank Schultz was in the Schmidt drug store and got a twenty-dollar bill changed. Mr. Flocken was unable to tell when it was and could not fix the date.

George Tipton, who signed the affidavit for the arrest of Steele and Dunlap, testified that he saw a man following Mrs. Scranton the night of the murder, but did not identify him as Dunlap.

Elmer Patten, who was with Steele when the body of Mrs. Scranton was found, was placed on the stand and told of finding it. None of his testimony incriminated Steele. According to Patten's testimony Steele's actions on the night of the murder were about the same as those of other people who were near the scene. Patten said Steele was in a meeting at the master mechanic's office at the beginning and also when the meeting closed.

Mrs. Goldie Fosnaught, Mrs. L. B. Lessig, Mrs. Edna Leeper, Mrs. Agnes Sosey and Patrolman John Wren were called yesterday afternoon. All their testimony went to the facts about the murder. None of their testimony connected either Steele or Dunlap with the crime.

Then from the *Bucyrus News Forum* on Tuesday, June 10, 1919, we have this brief headline and article: "Dunlap's Hearing Was Postponed Until Today."

Detectives Edward Dorward and George Tipton of Marion, the parties who caused the arrest of "Dr." Harry E. Dunlap of this city in connection with the Rosa Scranton murder, were in the city Saturday looking up evidence.

The preliminary hearing for Dunlap was postponed from Saturday until Monday afternoon at 3 o'clock. The detectives stated that they would develop some startling information at the hearing.

Also from the *Bucyrus News Forum* on Tuesday, June 10, 1919, there was this headline and small article: "Dunlap Given Hearing—Local Man Is Witness."

George Willie, local drayman, was called o Marion this afternoon as a witness in the preliminary hearing of Harry E. Dunlap, Bucyrus man, charged with the murder of Mrs. Rosa Scranton.

Dunlap was given a preliminary hearing Saturday in Justice Haberman's court. There were 32 witnesses subpoenaed to testify at the hearing.

Then the *Sandusky Register* had this brief announcement on June 10, 1919, with this brief headline: "Release 2 Suspects."
Marion, Ohio, June 9:

James Steele of Marion and Harry E. Dunlap of Bucyrus, who were arrested June 3 and charged with the murder of Mrs. Rosa Scranton near her home in Marion January 29, were released from custody today following a preliminary hearing before Justice C. W. Haberman. Clyde Scranton, husband of the murdered woman, will appear for a hearing Wednesday.

Reported in the *Mansfield News Journal* also on Tuesday, June 10, 1919, was this article with a bold headline: "TRUTH DISTORTED, PROSECUTOR SAID." "In Asking for Full Exoneration of Men Being Tried ON Murder Charge."
Marion, June 10:

Court attaches said today that never before in the history of local courts was a scene staged like that late yesterday afternoon when special prosecutor James E. Eymon, upon his own motion, asked that the presiding judge exonerate the two prisoners, Dr. Harry Dunlap of Bucyrus and James Steele, Marion, Erie railroad worker charged with the murder January 29 of Mrs. Clyde Scranton, 26.

"There is not on scintilla of evidence to show that these two men are guilty," said Prosecutor Eymon at the close of his witnesses testimony at the preliminary hearing of Dunlap and Steele.

These witnesses told here on the stand a very different story than they told us. I don't know whether they became rattled or whether they just lied, but I do know that according to the evidence adduced here these men charged with such a serious offense as murder are in no degree implicated whatever, and so I ask the court to discharge them and fully exonerate them in the eyes of the public. There should be some way to reach folks who so distort the truth.

Justice Haberman not only discharged Steele and Dunlap but fixed the bond of Clyde Scranton, husband of the murdered woman also held for her murder, at $5,000 and released him on a personal bond to appear for his preliminary hearing Wednesday.

The *Marion Daily Star* reported on June 11, 1919, a small item with this headline: "Will Remain in Bucyrus"

"Dr." Harry Dunlap, of Bucyrus, who was exonerated of the charge of the first-degree murder of Mrs. Clyde Scranton in Justice Charles Haberman's court late Monday afternoon only smiled when a reporter from the *Bucyrus Telegraph* asked him about the quantity of letters found in his trunk at his rooming house on west Mary street. Dunlap said the letters were all from women relatives. The *Bucyrus Telegraph* states Dunlap is planning to move his rooming quarters but will remain in Bucyrus.

Also found in the *Marion Daily Star* on June 11, 1919, was the article with these headlines: "WOMAN ACTS AS HER OWN LAWYER IN COURT TODAY" followed by "When Alleged Wife-Slayer's Preliminary Hearing Opens" then "SCRANTON'S ATTORNEY OBJECTS TO QUESTIONING" and "Prosecutor Young Says He Can't Be Prosecutor and Witness. Unusual Court Affair."

Mrs. M. E. Fritzinger, a private detective, who signed the affidavit for the arrest of Clyde Scranton, charging him with first-degree murder of his wife, the night of January 29, is conducting the examination of her own witnesses without any legal assistance before Justice Charles W. Haberman in the common pleas courtroom this afternoon. Scranton's preliminary hearing opened at 1:30 o'clock.

Prosecutor Hector S. Young, who was the first witness called this afternoon, said, when Mrs. Fritzinger began to question him, that he could not very well act as judge, prosecutor and witness. Mrs. Fritzinger was hampered by her lack of knowledge of legal procedure but struggled gravely in the work that ordinarily requires the services of skilled lawyers.

Attorney James H. Eymon, counsel for Mr. Scranton, objected to nearly every question asked by Mrs. Fritzinger. Mrs. Fritzinger introduced a paper writing, which she had turned over to

Prosecutor Young while she was working on the case for him, and started questioning him regarding it.

All the questions were objected to by counsel for the defendant. Mrs. Fritzinger finally excused Mr. Young and called Mrs. L. B. Lessig, who had signed the paper writing.

Mrs. Fritzinger's questions to Mrs. Lessig were objected to by counsel for the defendant on the ground that Mrs. Lessig was Mrs. Fritzinger's witness and she had no right to cross-examine her or doubt her statements.

Mrs. Fritzinger finally asked Mrs. Lessig to tell all she knew about the murder from the time she went to the Scranton home the morning of the murder until the time of finding the body.

Mrs. Lessig began to tell the details of the facts and events surrounding the murder of Mrs. Scranton, told by her at the preliminary hearing of James Steele, an Erie roundhouse employee and "Dr." Harry Dunlap of Bucyrus, who were exonerated of the charge of the first-degree-murder of Mrs. Scranton last Monday afternoon.

A large number of witnesses have been called by Mrs. Fritzinger to testify on the case.

Also from the June 11, 1919, *Marion Daily Star*, we have this small item with this headline: "CASE AGAINST SCRANTON IS DISMISSED TODAY" followed by "On the Motion of Mrs. Fritzinger, Who files Affidavit."

On the motion of Mrs. E. M. Fritzinger, the case against Clyde Scranton was dismissed this afternoon. Mrs. Fritzinger stating she did so on account of lack of cooperation on the part of the state. Mrs. Fritzinger had charged Scranton with murdering his wife.

Then in the *Marion Daily Star* on Thursday, June 12, 1919, this article appeared with these headlines: "COLLAPSE OF SCRANTON CASE LATE YESTERDAY" followed by "Details of Sudden Ending of Preliminary Hearing" then by "JUSTICE TELLS WOMAN HE'LL DISMISS CASE" and "Then Mrs. Fritzinger Asks For Dismissal—Statements of Young and Eymon."

"I have concluded to ask for the dismissal of this case, because I don't believe I have the cooperation of the state," Mrs. M. E. Fritzinger, a private detective, who caused the arrest of Clyde

Scranton for the murder of his wife the night of January 29, stated to Justice Charles W. Haberman late yesterday afternoon at the preliminary hearing of Scranton.

The statement came as a climax to a sensational court scene. Mrs. Fritzinger had struggled for several hours as her own lawyer before the court in an effort to bring out her evidence and practically every step of the way was blocked by legal objections by Scranton's attorney, James H. Eymon.

At the conclusion of the testimony Mrs. Fritzinger and Prosecutor Young went to the bench and had a conversation with Justice Haberman. The justice told her he was going to dismiss the case. This was the straw that broke the camel's back.

Mrs. Fritzinger stepped back to the trial table, looking the court square in the face, asked for dismissal of the case.

All during the afternoon Mrs. Fritzinger had bravely battled all kinds of legal trouble in putting on her own case. She was forced to examine all her witnesses and not knowing legal procedure she encountered innumerable legal difficulties. Nearly all her questions were objected to by Scranton's attorney, James Eymon, on technical grounds.

Justice Haberman did not rule on any of the objections, as Mrs. Fritzinger would ask another question or argue with counsel about the way the question was stated, before the court would have time to give a ruling on the objection.

The court-room was crowded with spectators who enjoyed the battle between Mrs. Fritzinger and Attorney Eymon. The court was forced to call for order several times.

Following Mrs. Fritzinger's statement Attorney Eymon rose and said: "We know the prosecutor well enough to know that criminals don't escape him when here is probable guilt, but he doesn't want to punish people when they shouldn't be, and he doesn't.

"In dismissing the case at the request of the prosecution it is hoped that some stain may be laid on the head of the prosecutor. We people of Marion county know who is in Marion county and we don't have to have people from Columbus tell us about the prosecuting attorney and we insist the defendant be dismissed because of the lack of any evidence pointing toward his guilt."

Prosecutor Young then arose and said to the court: "Seemingly I am getting involved in this case. I will say the prosecuting witness, Mrs. Fritzinger, was at one time in my employ, making an investigation in this case and she reported to me when she was in my employ and by the findings and reports made to me at that time I did not think the evidence sufficient to file an affidavit against anyone."

"She has not reported to me since leaving my employ and I don't know what evidence she has found, but if the evidence adduced was procured when she was in my employ I am still of the opinion there is no evidence to show any guilt of Scranton in the case."

Justice Haberman following the prosecutors statement promptly dismissed the charge against Scranton and Scranton promptly left the courtroom completely exonerated.

The *Bucyrus News Forum* reported on June 13, 1919, this news with this headline: "Clyde Scranton Freed From Murder Charges." Marion, June 12:

Clyde Scranton, arrested on charge of murder of his wife, Mrs. Rosa Scranton, on the evening of January 29, walked forth from the hearing held Wednesday afternoon a free man. The tale about the finding of the hair switch of Mrs. Scranton and the character of the food found in the windpipe of the dead woman fell to the ground and did not materialize in the evidence offered as did also those mysterious colored men.

Roy Kalow and Wilson who were reported to have seen Mrs. Scranton enter her home before the hour of her supposed murder and today the mystery of the murder of Mrs. Scranton is more deeply shrouded than ever.

Mrs. M. E. Fritzinger, a private detective, who signed the affidavit for the arrest of Clyde Scranton conducted the examination of her own witnesses without any legal assistance before Justice Charles W. Haberman in the common pleas court room.

A large number of witnesses had been called by Mrs. Fritzinger to testify on the case.

Also on June 13, 1919, in the *Bucyrus News Forum* appeared this headline and article: "Court Exonerates Dr. Harry Dunlap In Marion Murder."

Exonerated and cleared from all charges, after being apprehended and held on a charge of first-degree murder, Harry Dunlap of Bucyrus, known to Bucyrus people as Dr. Harry E. Dunlap, is home again.

"Doc" Dunlap is not kicking however about having been hauled before Justice Charles W. Haberman in the common pleas courtroom in the Marion county court house. "It might have been worse," was his spirit. Although the encounter with the hands of the law was not a very delightful experience, he is today a free man, and he might have been held several months before he gained his freedom.

Having been taken into custody last Tuesday on the charge of having been implicated in the murder of Mrs. Clyde Scranton, of Marion, on the night of January 29th, he was given a preliminary hearing and discharged. L. C. Feighner, attorney for Dunlap and Stenographer A. B. Bradstock, left for Marion Monday afternoon and represented Dunlap in the preliminary hearing set for 1 p. m.

After all the evidence was brought out by State Attorney James Eymon, Dunlap was exonerated. Each witness was placed on the stand and cross examined by Feighner, and as none of the testimony was of a convicting nature, Attorney Eyman himself recommended Dunlap's discharge.

The first witness called was Mrs. Frank Schultz of North Greenwood street, at whose home it is claimed Dunlap was the night of the murder.

Mrs. Schultz described Dunlap coming to the home about 6 o'clock in the evening. She said he seemed very nervous. She testified Dunlap said he came to Marion from Bucyrus on the car, but didn't say what time he arrived there. He told the Schultz family he was sick and had come for medicine, Mrs. Shultz testified.

Mrs. Schultz testified Dunlap mentioned in a conversation at the Schultz home he met an insurance woman on the car. Mrs. Schultz said he did not say who it was but said she was "a nice looking woman." She said she did not think he meant Mrs. Scranton. She said he remained at the Schultz home a half hour.

The witnesses testified Dunlap then left with Mr. Schultz and went down town to a drug store. Mrs. Schultz said her son John was at home when Dunlap was there. When asked where John was now Mrs. Schultz said she did not know.

In the examination, which was conducted by Attorney James H. Eymon, Mrs. Schultz placed the date when Dunlap was at her home on January 27.

Sheriff James F. Ullom was the next witness called. He testified Dunlap told him in the presence of other persons that he came to Marion January 29 on the 8 o'clock interurban car from Bucyrus and left on the 9 o'clock car.

Sheriff Ullom testified Dunlap said he came here to see a doctor whose name he could not remember. He testified Dunlap accounted for every minute of his time while in Marion and when it was added up it totaled two hours.

Sheriff Ullom testified Dunlap said he got off the car and went to a grocery and he inquired where the doctor lived. He said Dunlap told him he gave a boy 25 or 50 cents to take him to the Schultz home. Dunlap told the sheriff the exact time he was at each place and his every movement while in Marion.

Dunlap suffered a nervous collapse late Saturday afternoon following a grilling by detectives working on the case. Dunlap's condition became so bad Sheriff James F. Ullom was forced to call a physician. Dunlap recovered somewhat yesterday, but a doctor again waited on him yesterday morning. For a time Saturday afternoon, Sheriff Ullom said it was feared that Dunlap would die.

The hearing of Clyde Scranton, husband of the murdered woman, which was to have been held Monday morning at 9 o'clock in Justice Charles W. Haberman's court, was continued until Wednesday morning. The continuance was given at the request of Mrs. M. E. Fritzinger, a detective who caused the arrest of Scranton.

Mrs. Fritzinger stated to the court that she was unable to get some of her important witnesses here this morning in time for the hearing.

CHAPTER **13**

The Baby Rita

You, the reader, must have noticed by now that there has never been a mention of motive presented in this murder of Mrs. Rose Belle Scranton. In gathering information for this book, I have heard, through unsupported testimony, that Mr. Scranton may have thought he had a motive for the murder of his wife. That unsupported testimony suggested that Clyde Scranton's youngest child, eight-month old Rita Mae Scranton, was not fathered by him but was the result of a relationship between his wife and an unidentified person. This theory was supported, if you can make the connection, by the next two articles I found in the *Marion Daily Star.*

From the Wednesday, April 9, 1919, *Marion Daily Star,* we have this headline and article: "AUTHORITIES DENY ASK BODY BE EXHUMED" then "No Symptoms of Poisoning in Scranton Babe's Death" and "MARION OFFICIALS SAY ABOUT CINCINNATI STORY." Which was followed by "May Be Woman Detective, Formerly Employed by Prosecutor, Is Responsible for it."

A telegram from Cincinnati to the Star says that Marion county authorities were today granted permission from the Hamilton county authorities to exhume the body of eight-months-old Rita Scranton, who died in Cincinnati some time ago and was brought to Marion and buried.

Following the murder of Mrs. Clyde Scranton, the mother of the child, here, January 29, the baby, with an older sister, was taken to Cincinnati, where the baby was placed in an institution and died March 24. Bronchial pneumonia was given as the cause of death.

The telegram states that Marion authorities claimed symptoms of poisoning were found when the body reached here and that the other child being cared for in Marion, is now ill.

Investigation today discloses that none of the local authorities has asked permission to have the body exhumed. Prosecuting Attorney Hector S. Young, Police Chief J. W. Thompson and Coroner C. L. Baker stated that they had not asked permission to have the body exhumed and knew nothing of the move. All state there were no symptoms of poisoning.

A woman detective was employed by Prosecutor Young to work on another case shortly after the Scranton murder. A few days ago she announced she was going to Cincinnati, and it may be that she held out that she represented local authorities. But it is not understood why, were the body to be exhumed, it would be necessary to consult Hamilton county authorities.

The following day, in the *Marion Daily Star* on Thursday, April 10, 1919, this appeared: "REQUEST TO EXHUME SCRANTON BABY'S BODY" then "Denied by Hamilton county Authorities."

A special telegram to the Star from Cincinnati today says that Mrs. M. E. Fritzinger, the woman detective formerly employed by Prosecuting Attorney Hector S. Young in the murder of Mrs. Clyde Scranton, January 29, made the request of Hamilton county authorization yesterday to exhume the body of eight-month-old Rita Scranton who died in an institution at Cincinnati March 26 and was buried here. Today's telegram says further that the woman represented herself to be from Prosecutor Young's office, and this is emphatically denied by the Prosecutor. Mrs. Fritzinger told Prosecutor Capelle and Coroner Bauer at Cincinnati there were symptoms of poisoning in connection with the baby's death, though the doctor's certificate in Cincinnati showed that the child died of bronchial pneumonia. She also said, according to the Star's message from Cincinnati today, that another child is ill with the symptoms of poisoning. Both of these statements are untrue, local authorities say.

Permission to exhume the body was denied by the Hamilton county authorities. Prosecutor Capelle advised Mrs. Fritzinger take the matter up with the Attorney General. "I would not have authority to order the body exhumed." Prosecutor Capelle is quoted as saying, "If the prosecutor in Marion is unable or unwilling to make such an order the next higher authority would be the state attorney general."

"There is no evidence to warrant such a thing as exhuming the child's body" Prosecutor Young says.

CHAPTER 14

More about George Washington Warner AKA Esque

As you may remember, Esque Warner was the prime suspect for Mrs. Scranton's murder for something like a week or two after her murder. But after reading about him and the events that followed, I was convinced he had nothing to do with it. Also you may recall, Esque pled guilty to an assault with intent to rape charge and received an "indeterminate" sentence in the Mansfield Reformatory for that crime. He was incarcerated in the Mansfield Reformatory on February 14, 1919, to begin his "indeterminate" sentence.

I investigated this sentencing and Esque's time served and discovered that he was paroled on January 15, 1921, having served twenty-nine days short of two years. Then he was released from his sentence on March 15, 1922.

Esque was born in Mt. Pleasant, Tennessee, on August 25, 1898; lived at home until 1915, and had a third-grade education. His occupation was listed as laborer. He was five feet four inches tall and weighed 140 pounds. Esque had been previously incarcerated in Youngstown, Ohio, in 1917 for being drunk, then again in 1918 for fighting. His sheet also says he used intoxicating liquors, smokes cigarettes and cigars, and chews tobacco. I can't help but wonder about Esque.

CHAPTER 15

More about "Dr." Dunlap

From the *Mansfield News* on Thursday, July 31, 1919, we have this headline and article: "MYSTERIOUS DR. DUNLAP FASCINATES LOCAL GIRL" then this smaller headline "Wife Tells, in Divorce Court, of Night of Horror Spent at Home of Sister" then in capital letters again "SCREENED HOME IN CANADIAN WILDS" then "Husband Charges Wise Family All Against Him; Praises First Wife Highly."

Testimony of the most sensational sort, embracing both the natural and the spiritual world, feature the divorce case of Mary Wise Dunlap against Dr. Harry Dunlap, which is being heard common pleas court today by Judge Galbraith. Mrs. Dunlap is represented by Attorney A. S. Beach and Attorney Jonas Feightner of Bucyrus represents Dr. Dunlap.

Dr. Harry Dunlap of Bucyrus and Miss Mary Wise of East Second street, this city, were married after an acquaintance of just 43 hours. Dr. Dunlap says he met Miss Wise on a train coming from Toledo and that she exercised a strange fascination over him. He came on to this city with his new acquaintance and married her.

Mrs. Dunlap testified on the witness stand this morning that she never had a chance to have young men call on her as other girls had. Dr. Dunlap stated, off the stand, she had told him the same thing on the train. He says her story touched him and he proposed marriage to her.

Mrs. Dunlap says she told her new acquaintance she would like to find out more about him. She continued that he told her he was an osteopath physician and a Christian, and asked her what more she could want. He also assured her that he could support her. The couple went to the home of Mrs. Earl DeHart, sister of Mrs. Dunlap, where they continued their whirlwind courtship. Mrs. Dunlap says she was accompanying the doctor to the interurban station the next day, he intending to go back to Bucyrus.

Before reaching the interurban station, Mrs. Dunlap says her suitor proposed they get married at once, which they did. The wife says her husband gave his age 25 and his occupation as an osteopath physician. She said as soon as the ceremony was over, the bridegroom proposed to buy her a new pair of shoes, as he said he wanted her to look nice.

The newly weds went again to the DeHart home where they announced their marriage. Mrs. Dunlap says her sister proposed that she invite some people in and that they have a belling. This was the first time the bridegroom displayed one of his "fits" as his wife terms them. She says he became very excited and exclaimed, "You are going to get the police and the detectives after me. This is a hornet's nest you have gotten me into."

The wife says her husband was also accusing her of getting the police and detectives on his trail. She says he would then grow bolder and on one occasion threatened to kill Mayor Brunner, the bellers and all the police force.

"He put a revolver and a razor under his pillow when we went to bed at my sister's" Mrs. Dunlap continued. "He made a proposition to me, so terrible, I can not repeat it."

"Was this proposition unnatural?" Judge Galbraith asked.

"O, it was worse than unnatural," Mrs. Dunlap exclaimed. "Then he choked me and told me I had to go to Canada and live with other men. He told me he had a house, all screened in, and that I would be kept there. He then threatened to kill me and I screamed. My sister came into the room and stayed with us the remainder of the night. He choked me to keep me from telling my sister all."

"I had the flu and was sick." Dr. Dunlap said he would go and get some medicine for me. He went out and when he returned, he had a bottle of medicine with the label of a local doctor. I took one dose of the medicine and immediately became stiff. It seemed to affect my heart."

This testimony was corroborated by Mrs. Dehart. Mrs. Dunlap testified that when they went to her mother's home the next day, her husband got down on his knees, telling her mother he was sorry he had choked Mary and asked for forgiveness. His strange actions continued that day, the wife claims. She said her husband was always talking about police and detectives.

She said he threatened to take her to the mayor of Bucyrus. Mrs. Dunlap says she suggested going to Mayor Brunner as she was acquainted with him. She said her husband offered to give her $400 if she would not tell all she knew. Then he raised the offer to $1000. She says they met the mayor on the street, but the worst she told him was that she married hastily.

Mrs. Dunlap and Mrs. DeHart said Dr. Dunlap told them he always prayed with the women patients who came to him, then asked them to disrobe. "I accused him of being a white slave crook and told him a million dollars would not tempt me to lead the kind of life he wanted to take me to in the screened house in Canada," Mrs. Dulap testified.

"I told him I would not go to Bucyrus with him. Before he started he asked mama to make some ginger tea for him. After he left, he was continually sending special delivery letters, telegrams, calling me on the telephone or writing to me. The letters usually contained references to spiritualism. I told him that spiritualism was the work of the devil," was part of the testimony of Mrs. Dunlap.

Mrs. DeHart said he told her if he had met her before he met Mary, he would have married her.

Dr. Dunlap, the man of mystery, did not come into the courtroom, but remained out in the corridor. He will be recalled as one of the several suspects in connection with the unsolved murder of Mrs. Pearl [2] Scranton at Marion last winter. Mrs. Scranton had been accompanied home from Bucyrus by Dr. Dunlap the evening she was murdered, it was claimed. Dr. Dunlap was later released as proof enough to hold him in connection with the murder was lacking.

He is a man of rather imposing appearance, with nothing uncanny in his demeanor. He protests that he still loves his wife, loves her almost as much as he did his first wife.

---

2   This is an error by the reporter. Pearl is Rose Belle.

"There is the purest and sweetest woman that ever lived," Dr. Dunlap stated as he showed a picture of a young woman who, he says was his first wife. "We lived together 18 months. Her mother and sister lived with us. My mother-in-law would have come here to testify for me, if I had wanted her. I do not think I will take the stand."

"There is something fascinating about Mary Wise. She put it all over me when she told me her hard luck story on the train. I told her I was not married and I would marry her and take care of her. She had been sick with the flu before we were married. Her sister cooked a chicken for supper and it made both of us sick. I was stronger than she and recovered quicker. There is nothing to the stories she is telling her folks against me."

Dr. Dunlap denies the episode of the gun and the razor. He claims the only razor he had was a safety razor and that was in his grip. He also denies choking his bride. Mrs. Dunlap says he would not let her out of his sight that night or the next day for fear she would tell what she knew.

"I know something I would not tell anyone in the world," Dr. Dunlap declared. What this secret is or whom it concerns, he did not say. He claims he wishes his wife well and believes all would have been well, had her people not mingled in their affairs. He reiterated his statement that Mary Wise has a strange fascination for him, the same he seemed to have at first, for her. The husband proclaims his wife an innocent and most unusual girl. "Everything has been as straight as a string in our relations," he says.

Although Dr. Dunlap assured his wife, in one of the letters written after their marriage, that he had given up spiritualism, he testified at the hearing on temporary alimony, that he is a divine healer. Mrs. Dunlap and one of her sisters made a trip to Bucyrus and visited his office. The woman in charge told them she knew some things that would send her employer to the penitentiary, Mrs. Dunlap says.

"We were sitting on the sofa the first night he came to see me, and Dr. Dunlap kept looking at me in such a strange way, my mind became a blank," Mrs. Dunlap testified. She also testified of the constant fear her husband had of detectives.

Another witness testified of meeting Dr. Dunlap on the train, and of the strange way he looked at her. She said he finally told her she had defective eyes, but he could take care of her. The witness said Dr. Dunlap told her she would have to disrobe. None of the witnesses was cross examined by the attorney for the defense.

Mrs. Dunlap testified further that the first day of their marriage, her husband told her of this mysterious home in Canada, secure from observation, where she would be expected to sustain relations with other men.

After hearing the testimony, Judge Galbraith granted Mrs. Dunlap a divorce on the grounds of fraudulent contract. The wife refused to accept any alimony, declaring Dunlap's money is tainted. She is restored to her maiden name, Mary Wise.

Also on Thursday, July 31, 1919, the *Marion Daily Star* had this to say with these headlines: "CLAIRVOYANT DUNLAP IS SUED FOR DIVORCE," then "Says He Threatened To Make Her White Slave," and "SENSATIONAL SUIT IN RICHLAND COUNTY TODAY," and finally, "Meet on Train, Wed Forty-Three Hours Later_Figures in the Scranton Murder."

Mrs. Mary Dunlap, wife of "Dr." Harry Dunlap, clairvoyant, who was arrested and brought to this city in connection with the murder of the late Mrs. Clyde Scranton, today brought suit for a divorce in the Richland county courts, according to information received today from Mansfield. Mrs. Dunlap brings some sensational charges against her husband, to whom she was married in February after an acquaintanceship of forty-three hours.

The couple became acquainted on board a train. Before her marriage Mrs. Dunlap was Miss Mary Wise of Mansfield.

In her petition, Mrs. Dunlap says her husband choked her and that she was compelled to call her sister to prevent Dunlap from killing her. She declares that he threatened to kill the mayor of Mansfield and all the police of that city. He threatened to take her to a mysterious home he had in Canada, she says, where he intended to make her a "white slave" of her.

Mrs. Dunlap says "Dr." Dunlap had his patients disrobe before he made examinations. She also brings many other charges in her petitions.

Then on Friday, August 1, 1919, the *Marion Daily Star* followed up with this report and headline: "MRS. HARRY E. DUNLAP IS AWARDED A

DIVORCE" followed by this headline, "Refuses Alimony, Saying Dunlap's Money is Tainted."

Mrs. Mary Wise Dunlap was granted a divorce yesterday from "Dr." Harry E. Dunlap, Bucyrus clairvoyant, in the common pleas court of Richland county, at Mansfield by Judge Galbraith. "Dr." Dunlap was arrested and brought to this city a few weeks ago in connection with the murder of the late Mrs. Clyde Scranton but was later exonerated. The couple were married after an acquaintance of forty-three hours. They met on a train going from Toledo to Mansfield last February. Dunlap accompanied Miss Wise to the latter city and married her according to his statement. Mrs. Dunlap returned alimony, declaring that Dunlap's money was "tainted."

Mrs. Dunlap testified on the witness stand that she had never had a chance to have young men visit her as other girls had. Dunlap said she told him the same thing on the train and that he took pity on her and married her. He said that her story so touched him that he proposed marriage to her. Mrs. Dunlap testified that Dr. Dunlap told her he was an osteopath physician and a Christian and assured her that he could support her when she hesitated about accepting him immediately after his proposal of marriage.

Mrs. Dunlap testified that Dunlap insisted upon getting married as soon as they reached Mansfield, which they did. The newlyweds went at once to the home of Mrs. Dunlap's sister, who proposed inviting some friends in honor of the bride and groom. The groom at once displayed one of his "fits," according to Mrs. Dunlap. He became very excited and exclaimed "you are going to get the police and detectives after me." She says he put a revolver and razor under his pillow when they went to bed. Mrs. Dunlap testifies that when she had the "flu," Dunlap gave her some medicine which affected her strangely.

Dr. Dunlap, who was known in Mansfield as "the man of mystery," did not go into the courtroom. During the trial he remained in the corridor and protested that he still loved his wife almost as much as he did his first wife.

CHAPTER 16

More about Clyde Scranton

After losing his wife and infant daughter, Clyde Scranton remarried, started another family, and lived in the same home at 265 Cass Avenue. Clyde and his first wife, Rose Belle, had three children: Ruth, who was about four at the time of the murder; Frances, about two at the time of the murder; and Rita, the infant who died at eight months old in April 1919, a little over two months after the murder.

Clyde remarried to Selora and they had three children together: Mary, Christine, and Claudine. Clyde then was tragically killed in a motor vehicle accident in Wayne County on March 4, 1934.

DEPARTMENT OF HEALTH
DIVISION OF VITAL STATISTICS
CERTIFICATE OF DEATH

1 PLACE OF DEATH
County *Wayne*
Registration District No. *1353*
File No. *_____*

Township *Canaan*
Primary Registration District No. *6077*
Registered No. *5*

or Village _____ No. _____ St. _____ Ward

or City of _____

Length of residence in city _____ (If death occurred in a hospital or institution, give its name instead of street and number)

Now long in U. S. if of foreign birth? _____

2 FULL NAME *Clyde Paul Scranton*

(a) Residence *265 Case ave, Marion O* Ward

Did Deceased Serve in
U. S. Navy or Army _____

(If nonresident give city or town and State)

PERSONAL AND STATISTICAL PARTICULARS | MEDICAL CERTIFICATE OF DEATH

3 SEX *Male*
4 COLOR OR RACE *White*
5 Single, Married, Widowed *Married*

5a. If married, widowed, or divorced
HUSBAND of
(or) WIFE of *Zetara Fox Scranton*

6 DATE OF BIRTH *June 18-1887*

7 AGE Years *47* Months _____ Days _____ IF LESS than 1 day, ...hrs. ...min.

OCCUPATION
8 Trade, profession, or particular kind of work done *Laborer*
9 Industry or business in which work was done *CWA* ... *How*
10 Date deceased last worked at this occupation _____ Total time (years) spent in this

11 BIRTHPLACE (city or town) *Marion Co*
(State or country) *Ohio*

FATHER
12 NAME *Michael Scranton*
13 BIRTHPLACE (city or town) *Ohio*
(State or country)

MOTHER
14 MAIDEN NAME *Eva Brun*
15 BIRTHPLACE (city or town) *Ohio*
(State or country)

16 INFORMANT *Miss Ethel McDougal*
(Address) *541 Center, Marion O*

17 BURIAL, CREMATION, OR REMOVAL
Place *Marion* Date *3 8 34*

18 UNDERTAKER *John C Murray*
(Address) *Creston*

18a. Was body embalmed *yes* Embalmer's ... *35741 A*

20 FILED *Mar 4 1934* *W H Bechtel* Registrar

21 DATE OF DEATH (month, day, and year) *Mar 4, 1934*

22 I HEREBY CERTIFY, That I attended deceased from _____ to _____

that I last saw *dead 3/4* *1934* death is said

to have occurred on the date stated above at *2:30 P m*

The PRINCIPAL CAUSE OF DEATH and related causes of importance in order of onset were as follows:
Date of onset *3/4/34*

Traumatic killed instantly
on an automobile accident
while riding in an automobile
on CCC Highway south of Creston, O

CONTRIBUTORY CAUSES of importance not related to principal cause:

none

Name of operation _____ Date of _____
What test confirmed diagnosis? *History* Was there an autopsy? *no*

23 If death was due to external causes (violence) fill in also the following:
Accident *3 Day of Mar* *1934*
Where did injury occur? *on public Highway*
(State or county)

Specify whether injury occurred in industry, in home, or in public place.
On public Highway

Manner of injury *automobile accident*

Nature of injury _____

24 Was disease or injury in any way related to occupation of deceased? *no*

If so, specify _____

(Signed) *Lyman A. Adams* M. D.
3/4 *1934* (Address) *Coroner Wayne Co*

PLACE OF DEATH.

County of *Hamilton*

Township of

or

Village of

City of *Cincinnati* (No. *Tennessee Av.* St. *13* Ward)

RETURNED 494

Registration District No.

Primary Registration District N *8227*

File No.

Registered N *2229*

19530

* FULL NAME *Rita Maria Scranton*

PERSONAL AND STATISTICAL PARTICULARS

SEX *F* | COLOR OR RACE *W* | SINGLE MARRIED WIDOWED OR DIVORCED (Write the word)

DATE OF BIRTH *7 18 1918*
(Month) (Day) (Year)

AGE *8* yrs. *6* mo. If LESS than 1 day, ... hrs. ... min.

OCCUPATION
(a) Trade, profession, or particular kind of work
(b) General nature of industry, business, or establishment in which employed (or employer)

BIRTHPLACE (State or country) *Marion, Ohio*

NAME OF FATHER *Clyde Scranton*

BIRTHPLACE OF FATHER (State or country) *Marion, Ohio*

MAIDEN NAME OF MOTHER *Rose Baker*

BIRTHPLACE OF MOTHER (State or country) *Marion, Ohio*

THE ABOVE IS TRUE TO THE BEST OF MY KNOWLEDGE

(Informant) *Nancy R. Lynn*

(Address) *385 East 8th St, City*

Filed *MAR 31 1919* *Lewellin Evans* Registrar

MEDICAL CERTIFICATE OF DEATH

DATE OF DEATH *3 24 1919*
(Month) (Day) (Year)

I HEREBY CERTIFY, That I attended deceased from *3 17 1919* to *3 24 1919* that I last saw her alive on *3 24 1919* and that death occurred, on the date stated above, at ... m.

The CAUSE OF DEATH was as follows:

Broncho Pneumonia

(Duration) yrs. mos. ds.

Contributory (Secondary)

(Duration)

(Signed) *J. Weiss* M.D.

3 28 (Address) *Norwood O.*

LENGTH OF RESIDENCE (For Hospitals, Institutions, Transients, or Recent Residents)

PLACE OF BURIAL OR REMOVAL *Marion Ohio*

DATE OF BURIAL *March 25 1919*

UNDERTAKER *John J. Gilligan*

ADDRESS

PLACE OF DEATH.

County of _Marion_

Township of _____   Registration District No. _811_   File No. _5264_

or

Village of _____   Primary Registration District No. _8369_   Registered No. _32_

City of _Marion_   (No. _265_ _Cass_ St., _____ Ward) [If death occurred in a hospital or institution, give its NAME instead of street and number.]

1 FULL NAME _Rose Belle Scranton_

PERSONAL AND STATISTICAL PARTICULARS	MEDICAL CERTIFICATE OF DEATH
3 SEX _F_ 4 COLOR OR RACE _W_ 5 SINGLE MARRIED WIDOWED OR DIVORCED (Write the word) _Married_	16 DATE OF DEATH _January 29_, 191_9_ (Month)(Day)(Year)
6 DATE OF BIRTH _Aug_ _5_, _1892_ (Month)(Day)(Year)	17 I HEREBY CERTIFY, That I attended deceased from _Jan 29_ 191_9_ to _January 29_, 191_9_
7 AGE _27_ yrs. _____ mos. _____ ds. IF LESS than 1 day, _____ hrs. or _____ min.	that I last saw h_____ alive on _____, 191_9_ and that death occurred, on the date stated above, at _11_ _m._ The CAUSE OF DEATH* was as follows:
8 OCCUPATION (a) Trade, profession, or particular kind of work _House wife_	_Concussion of Brain (Homicidal)_ _due to blow on head, (was found_
(b) General nature of industry, business, or establishment in which employed (or employer)	_was also found in trunk.)_
9 BIRTHPLACE (State or country) _Richwood Ohio_	(Duration) _____ yrs. _____ mos. _1_ ds.
PARENTS 10 NAME OF FATHER _Wm Baker_	Contributory (SECONDARY)
11 BIRTHPLACE OF FATHER (State or country) _U.S._	(Duration) _____ yrs. _____ mos. _____ ds. (Signed) _Frank W Murphy_ M.D.
12 MAIDEN NAME OF MOTHER _Not known_	_Jan 31_ 191_9_ (Address) _Marion O_
13 BIRTHPLACE OF MOTHER (State or country) _Ohio_	*State the DISEASE CAUSING DEATH, or, in deaths from VIOLENT CAUSES, state (1) MEANS of INJURY; and (2) whether ACCIDENTAL, SUICIDAL, or HOMICIDAL.
14 THE ABOVE IS TRUE TO THE BEST OF MY KNOWLEDGE	18 LENGTH OF RESIDENCE (For Hospitals, Institutions, Transients, or Recent Residents)
(Informant) _Clyde Scranton_	At place of death _____ yrs. _____ mos. _____ ds. In the State _____ yrs. _____ ds.
(Address) _Marion Ohio_	Where was disease contracted, if not at place of death? Former or usual residence
15	19 PLACE OF BURIAL OR REMOVAL DATE OF BURIAL
Filed _Jan 31_, 191_9_ _J L Lambu_ Registrar	_St Marys Cem_ _Jan 31_ 191_9_
11—3184	20 UNDERTAKER ADDRESS _Geo. Markus_ _Marion Ohio_

Epilogue

When I began to look into this story, this episode in Marion's history, I was motivated to find out more about the racial aspect that was so evident in the beginning. Yet as I continued to read the description of events that led from the tragic murder of Mrs. Rose Belle Scranton, I was intrigued by all the, what seemed to me, to be the only peripheral events around the main story. I soon believed that while the murder was the central event in this story, the racial aspect was in itself an equally tragic set of events.

While the murder and the racial aspects were upsetting, maybe more than just upsetting, I was impressed by the actions of the mayor of Marion and the actions of Marion's police chief, sheriff, and judge in moving to protect Esque Warner from the actions of the mob.

Certainly, Isaac Hill and "Dr." Harry Dunlap added to my interest in this story. And the supporting cast, the neighbors, the babysitter, Mrs. Christian, Miss Mary Wise, and Mrs. M. E. Fritzinger added to my interest, as well as the birth and death of Rita Scranton, the infant daughter of Rose and Clyde.

Perhaps the real murderer of Mrs. Scranton escaped notice, but I am inclined to think that the murderer was in our story somewhere. In any case, I hope you enjoyed reading this as much as I enjoyed putting this story together.

Phil Reid

INDEX

Edwards Brothers Malloy
Oxnard, CA USA
November 19, 2014